Salvador

For Partiers

RESTAURAÇÃO E REVITAL
DA FACULDADE DE MED
DO TERREIRO DE

©20004 Copyright Editora Solcat Ltda
All rights reserved - Editora Solcat Ltda.
Writer/Editor/Art Director: Cristiano Nogueira
Illustrations: Diego Avila Xavier & Felipe Moraes
Research: Ronaldo Alperin, Luis Felipe Nunes
Marketing: Ricardo dos Santos
Maps: Diego Avila Xavier
Photography: Cristiano Nogueira, Ronaldo Alperin & Bahia-Tursa (Jota Freitas)
Book design: Cristiano Nogueira
Logo design: Felipe Ferreira de Moraes

The editors of the book did their best to offer information that was up to date at the time of printing. However, some data is subject to change and the editors cannot accept responsibility for changes that have occured since the book's printing.

Readers interested in sending their suggestions, ideas or complaints can do so via email at support@salvadorforpartiers.com
or by writing to our postal address:

Solcat Editora
Rua Visconde de Pirajá 48 SL 702, Ipanema,
Rio de Janeiro , RJ CEP 22411-000, tel:21-2523-9857 USA: 1-312 546-4748
web: www.salvadorforpartiers.com

Part of "For Partiers" series of guides. Published and printed in Brazil by Editora Solcat Ltda. First Edition.

Nogueira, Cristiano
Salvador for Partiers / [texts and photography]
Cristiano Nogueira. -- Rio de Janeiro : Solcat Editora, 2004 --(For Partiers)

1. Salvador (BA) - Descrição e viagens - Guias
I. Título. II. Série

04-8513   CDD-918.1421

The Solcat team

CRISTIANO NOGUEIRA
Editor and writer.

FELIPE MORAES
Illustrator.

RONALDO ALPERIN
Chief researcher. Knows Salvador like the back of his hand.

DIEGO AVILA XAVIER
Map and photo-artist

LUIZ FELIPE MARTINS
Tourism research assistant

RICARDO DOS SANTOS
Marketing

THANKS
Milton, Emilia, Zeze, Zelia, Chuca, Nyala, Ronaldo, Saulo, Patricio Valle, Randy, Doug, Thomas, Willy, Octacilio, Orlando, Francisco, Rodrigo, Rose, Luis Fernando, Dan, John, Nathalie, Daniela, my trusty Canon Powershot S45, Brian, Ana Cristina and all the partners.

PHOTO CREDITS
Cristiano Nogueira, Ronaldo Alperin, Agência Globo, Biblioteca Nacional & Bahiatursa (designated by BT).

Salvador For Partiers

by Cristiano Nogueira

Check for updates at
www.salvadorforpartiers.com/updates.html

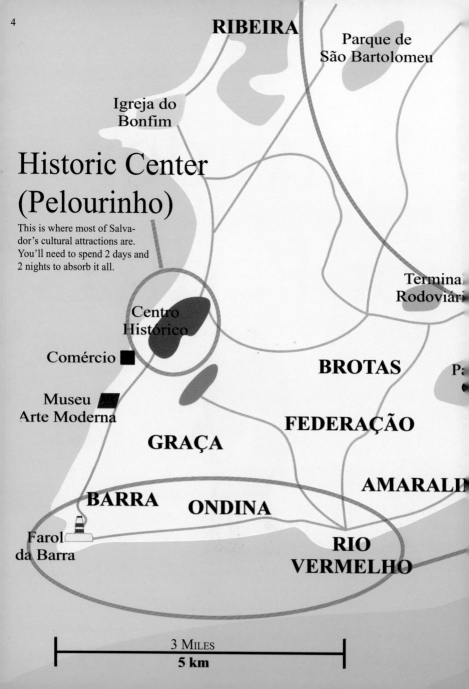

RIBEIRA

Parque de
São Bartolomeu

Igreja do
Bonfim

Historic Center
(Pelourinho)

This is where most of Salvador's cultural attractions are.
You'll need to spend 2 days and
2 nights to absorb it all.

Termina
Rodoviári

Centro
Histórico

Comércio

BROTAS

P

Museu
Arte Moderna

FEDERAÇÃO

GRAÇA

AMARALI

BARRA   **ONDINA**

Farol
da Barra

**RIO
VERMELHO**

3 Miles
5 km

Salvador at a Glance

Airport

Residential Burroughs

Mostly lower class or industrial neighbourhoods, with little to no touristic attractions.

ITAPUÃ

BOCA DO RIO

PIATÃ

Itapoan

A laid back neighbourhood, far from the city and close to the best beaches. Commonly used as reference point to designate the city's north-most area.

ARMAÇÃO

IGARA

COSTA AZUL

PITUBA

Ocean Beaches

A long stretch with various beaches, each better than the last the further north you go. Clubs, concert halls and restaurants evenly sprinkled over this zone.

Barra to Rio Vermelho

Most the hotels are located between these two neighbourhoods, since they are central to most visitors' tour activities: Rio Vermelho has many of the night spots, Barra has a beach and proximity to Pelourinho. Many restaurants are located in this zone.

ATLANTIC OCEAN

WHAT TO BRING

CLOTHES (ALL SEASONS)

Your choices should be light in weight and color, as black clothes is looked down upon in the Candomble religion, a popular faith in the city. Bring one set of nice clothes, as there are many trendy clubs and restaurants that require elegant attire.

List based on one week's stay:

3 Bermudas

1 Pants

7 underpants

4 T-shirts or short-sleeved shirts

1 long-sleeved shirt or sweater

1 pair of sandals or all-terrain shoes

1 pair social shoes

4 pairs of socks

1 light nylon rain jacket

EQUIPMENT

Sunglasses

Cheap watch

Digital camera (the smallest possible)

Disposable camera (for street events)

Anti-diarrhea medication

Toiletries (all types can be found here in case you forget)

Cap

Cellular phone: Check your provider's coverage first, as there are several carriers that work with GSM system, allowing you to buy a chip (US$17), credits and pay local rates.

MONEY

Cheap spending (eating at the hostel, few restaurants, no hard-core clubbing, basic tours): US$25 a day

Average spending (restaurants and street food, hostel or cheap hotel, most of the tours): US$50 a day

All-out living (nice hotel, restaurants, all the tours, clubbing, shopping, massages etc): US$80 a day

We suggest you bring US$300 in cash and the rest you can either pay with your credit card or withdraw from cash-machines around the city (most work with Cirrus). If you plan on making larger purchases, like precious stones, bring traveller's checks.

PETTY CASH POOL

If you are in a group, instead of each person in the group paying for their beer, for the taxi, for the entrance and other small stuff, we recommend for you to chose one person who will carry the petty cash. Each morning, each member chips in R$50...

IDS AND CARDS

Passport

Student ID or Driver's License

Tourist Visa

2 Credit Cards (Visa & Mastercard)

BEFORE FLYING TO BRAZIL

Call the closest Brazilian consulate and check with them on the required vaccines and visas. Listing of consulates around the world at:

http://www.brazil.org.uk/

WHAT YOU DON'T NEED TO BRING

Towel (use the hotel`s)

Safari Hat (please!)

Binoculars (available in jungle tours)

Swimming gear (please don`t wear US or European beach fashion in Brazil, you`ll stick out and get constantly bugged by vendors).

Snorkel (you can rent it)

Winter jacket

Laptop (use the internet cafes)

0 SALVADOR COMMANDMENTS

1 DON'T GET STUCK IN PELOURINHO

Pelourinho can be seen in two days and two nights. After that, devote your time to discovering the rest of the city and nearby towns.

2 DON'T WALK AROUND WITH JEWELRY

Ladies and gentlemen! This is not your turf, so no matter how much clout you have at home, it is not worth shit here. Necklaces, rings, expensive watches, bracelets etc. are not to be worn except when you are off to a swanky event or club. Otherwise, keep it down low.

3 DON'T ARGUE WITH COPS

The cops here are instructed to take action as opposed to discuss who is right. It doesn't matter who is right, who stole what from whom, or if you didn't know she was under 18. If they want to arrest you for anything, let them, then call your consulate. If they want to fine you for something you did, usually for a driving offence, (another reason to not drive), then it is up to your slickness to implore them out of giving you a ticket.

4 GET CHANGE FOR A 50

The surest way to end up in hell is to walk around with a R$50 note thinking the beer guy, the bus or taxi will have change. Whenever at a restaurant, shop or bar, pay with the R$50. 5 R$10 bills are worth more than a R$50.

7 DO GET A TOURIST GUIDE FOR CULTURAL TOURS

The tourist guide wants to enchant you with what they know about the city. The taxi driver wants to drive from A to B back to A and collect. Go with the guide even if costs twice the amount.

6 DON'T STAY FAR AWAY BECAUSE IT IS CHEAPER

Okay, you have a Brazilian connection you met back home or on the Internet. He is the one who begged you to come and you did. After arriving , you realize he lives in bumble fuck. What to do? Stay at his place and please him rather than enjoy the practicality of staying in Ipanema, as this Guide suggests? Or should you tell him that you want to explore Salvador by yourself during the day (while he works or goes to school) and that you two can hook up at night? Go for the second option. You will waste more time on cab traveling to and from his place.

7 DON'T TRY TO DRIVE

Don't rent a car and try to figure out Brazilian road signs. Ok, believe this: not even locals know how to get around this maze-like city. So unless you've got a very good excuse, don't try to drive around. One wrong turn and you can end up in the slums, being fined by the cops, or stuck in rush hour traffic. Even if your trip is all-expenses-paid, stick to taxis.

8 DON'T TRY THE PEPPERS

Your stomach is not used to Brazilian peppers. Even if you can handle them, your intestines are bound to react in an explosive way.

9 DON'T SKIMPT OUT

Hey! As soon as you arrive in Brazil you become 3 times as rich as back in the 1st World. Instead going on the cheap, why not live large at the nicer restaurants, tours, hotels and bars?

10 DON'T ENGAGE IN CONVERSATION WITH THE BEGGARS

When the street kid comes begging, just ignore them for a while then give them the no sign. If you engage in conversation (negotiation) with them, they can always start crying and you lose. The city also loses as you'll be cultivating an unwated activity.

Where to Stay: Pelourinho

Pelourinho is a great option for those looking to be located inside the historical center. Most of the pousadas (inns), hotels and hostels are in colonial houses with no elevators, swimming pools or any other fluff.

Laranjeiras Hostel $
One of the nicest hostels in Brazil, Laranjeiras is also well located in right in the middle of Pelourinho. One major advantage (as all hostel clients know) is that you group up with other travellers and do stuff together.
Rua da Ordem Terceira 13
www.laranjeirashostel.com.br
hi@laranjeirashostel.com.br

Quilombo do Pelo $$
Pousada perfectly located in a colonial building right above the action: half a block from everything in Pelourinho. Free internet. Jamaican cuisine.TV, boom box, safe and phone. AC optional.
Rua Alfredo de Brito 13, Centro Historico
322-4371
gobahia@hotmail.com
www.quilomboinbahia.com

Hotel Pelourinho
Rua Alfredo Brito , 20
243 – 2324
www.hotelpeourinho.cpm

Hotel Ilhéus
Ladeira da Praça , 4
322 – 7240
www.hotelilheus.com.br

Hotel Pousada Beija-flor
Rua Direita de Santo Antônio 259, Santo Antônio
Centro Histórico
241 – 2472
www.beijaflorpousada.com.br

Pousada da Mangueira
Ladeira da Saúde , 9 – Saúde
Centro Histórico
242 – 3926
www.pousadadamangueira.com.br

Albergue do Pelô
Rua do Passo , 5
242 – 8061
www.alberguedopelo.com.br

Pousada do Boqueirão
Rua Direita de Santo Antonio , 48
Santo Antonio Além do Carmo
(71) 241-2262
www.pousadaboqueirao.com.br

Red Fish Inn
Ladeira do Boqueirão , 1
Centro Histórico
(71) 243-8473
www.hotelredfish.com

Hotel do Forte
Rua Visconde de São Lourenço , 30
Campo Grande
(71) 329-5774
www.hoteldoforte.com.br

Hotel Campo Grande
Rua Forte de São Pedro , 50
Campo Grande
(71) 328-3011
www.hotelcampogrande.com.br

Tropical da Bahia Business & Vacation
Av. 7 de Setembro , 1537
Campo Grande
(71) 255-2000
www.tropicalhotel.com.br

Pousada das Flores
Rua Direita de Santo Antônio , 442
Santo Antônio Além do Carmo
(71) 243-1836
www.pflores.com.br

Pousada Villa Carmo
Rua do Carmo , 58
Santo Antônio Além do Carmo
(71) 241-3924
www.pousadavillacarmo.com.br

Quilombo do Pelô
Rua Alfredo de Brito , 13
Pelourinho
(71) 322-4371 / (71) 242-9859
www.quilombodopelo.hpg.com.br

Sofitel Salvador Pelourinho
Largo do Carmo
Pelourinho
(71) 0800-703-7000

Brazil area code = 55, Salvador city code= 71   For each $= upto R$50

MAP OF STUFF NEAR YOU

You can find basic stores in Pelourinho (drug store, convenience stores, internet cafe etc), but if you want larger stores like a super-market or shopping mall, you'll have to take a cab over to Graça, Barra or Federação.

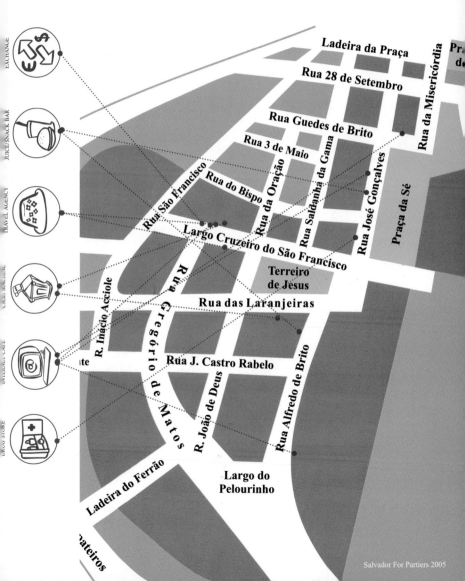

Where to Stay: East Coast

Another option ideal for those more interested in spending their time on the beach are the hotels along the east coast of Salvador. Hotels in Barra and Rio Vermelho have nice views and are close to lots of night spots. Itapua is closer to many of the nicer beaches. Most of these inns and hotels have all the expected conveniences and services.

Barra

Mansao Villa Verde $$$

7 Apts with kitchens and private bathrooms. Ideal for those staying over 1 week and under a month. Great location.
Willy Wolfgang (UK,GM, FR, PT)
Rua da Palmeira 190, Barra
www.villaverde-flats.com
admi@villaverde-flats.com
9134-6601

Bahia-prime.com $$$

Apartment rental site offering 50 apts in between Barra and Rio Vermelho. Prices start at R$1000/week for a one bedroom, up to $10,000 for fully equiped mansions.
Thomas (UK, GM,IT,SP,FR, PT)

Barra Turismo Hotel
Av Sete de Setembro 3691, Porto da Barra
264 – 0038
www.barraturismo.com.br

Albergue Casa da Barra
Rua Afonso Celso 447, Barra
264 – 1289
www.casadabarra.kit.net

Praiamar Hotel
Av Sete de Setembro 3577, Porto da Barra
264 – 0711
www.praiamarhotel.com.br

Âmbar Pousada
Rua Afonso Celso 485, Barra
264 – 6956 / 264 – 3791
www.ambarpousada.com.br

Albergue do Porto
Rua Barão de Sergy 197, Barra
264 – 6600 / 264 – 6452
www.alberguedoporto.com.br

Barra Praia Hotel
Rua Almirante Marquês de Leão 172, Barra
235 – 0193

Seara Praia Hotel
Rua Belo Horizonte 148, Jardim Brasil Barra
331 – 0105
www.searapraiahotel.com.br

Ondina

Ondina Praia Hotel
Av Oceânica 3033, Ondina
245 – 3454
www.ondinaplaza.com.br

Bahia Othon Palace
Avenida Oceânica 2294, Ondina
203 – 2000
www.hoteis-othon.com.br

Itapoan

Pousada Encanto de Itapoan $$$

Well groomed pousada with american size beds, swimming pool and high pressure showers.
Rua Nova Canaa 48, Farol de Itapoan
www.encantodeitapoan.com.br
info@encantodeitapoan.com.br

Brazil area code = 55, Salvador city code = 71   For each $= upto R$50

MAP OF STUFF

NEAR YOU

From Barra to Rio Vermelho, you can find most of the stores and services along the ocean drive. A few malls are sprinkled a few blocks in.

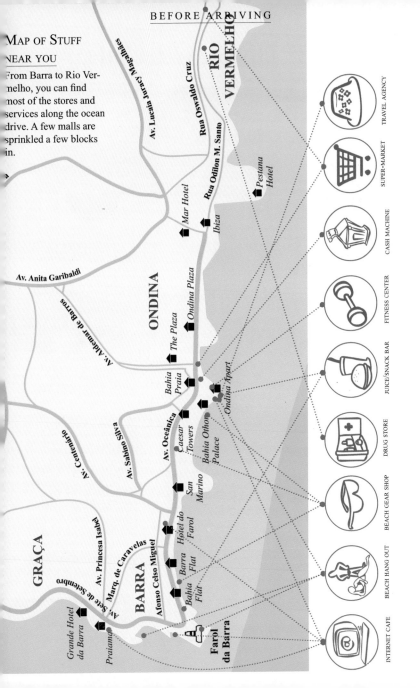

TRAVEL AGENCY

SUPER-MARKET

CASH MACHINE

FITNESS CENTER

JUICE/SNACK BAR

DRUG STORE

BEACH GEAR SHOP

BEACH HANG OUT

INTERNET CAFE

GETTING AROUND

TAXI

Getting around in Salvador is easy: just get in a cab! 1 out of every 3 cars is a taxi (or so it seems). What's more: it's cheap. You can go from Pelourinho to Rio Vermelho for about R$18 (US$7). From Pelourinho to Barra for about R$10. Just remember to ask the taxi driver if he knows how to get to where you want to go before you step in "voce sabe chegar no …. " pronounced "vo-say sa-bee shay-gar no [insert place here]…". If he doesn't know, take the next cab.

Most cabs like to drive tourists along the coast, as not only is it prettier but tourists get skeptical when they drive through inner city shourt cuts. When travelling between Rio Vermelho and Pelourinho, ask him to go "por dentro", through the middle, as that can save you R$10 each way.

If you are travelling longer distances, you can try to negotiate a price cheaper than the expected cost before stepping in the cab. You can usually knock off 10% to 20%.

One english -speaking cab driver we use is Villela:

Villela Cab
9105-9360

and Orlando (only portuguese spoken, but cheap deals)
Orlando Cab
9191-4526

CAR RENTALS

Renting a car is not the best option unless you have a Brazilian escort who will be driving you around. It does come very helpful if you are planning on visiting Praia do Forte or the north coast beaches, Porto Seguro or Itacare. Be sure to rent cars from reputable rental companies. Also opt for the company that does not hold R$800 in "calcao" (deductable) when you get insurance, otherwise, what's the point?

SELETIVO

A great option if you don't want to pay $50 from the Aiport to downtown. It goes along the ocean drive, giving access to most of the Hotels in Salvador between the Airport and Historic Center. Last stop, Praca da Se in Pelourinho.

They go for R$5 and run more frequently during rush hours.

BUS

The other less recommended transportation method is the public buses. Although a lot cheaper, these take longer (up to 95 minutes from Pelourinho to Itapua, where a cab would take 30 minutes) and are riskier, as crooks have been robbing buses, and the mob sets one or two on fire when angry at the government.

THINGS YOU'LL NEED TO GET

AT THE BEACH GEAR SHOP

Flip Flop Sandals

Brazilian fashion beach wear

Frescobol paddles

AT THE PHARMACY

Sun-screen and after-sun lotion (Aloe Vera)

Disposable camera

Hangover medicine "remedio para ressaca"

AT THE SUPER-MARKET

Toilet paper

Water Bottle

Snacks

WITH THE STREET VENDORS

Fake watch

Calling card (found at the news-stands, roughly R$5)

Fake SunGlasses

WHAT TO ALWAYS HAVE WITH YOU:

Reals ("Hey-ays") in small bills

Photo ID (not passport)

1 VISA credit card

Anti-diarhea medicine "remedio para desar-ranjo"

DAY OPTIONS

Culture: History

THE 90 SECOND HISTORY OF BRAZIL

For those of you who haven't done your research, here goes:

Brazilian history is closely parallel to that of the US: It was discovered in 1500 and soon colonized by the Portuguese.

First, brazil-wood was extracted for its red pigment. By 1600 the Portuguese were trying to cultivate the land with slave labor.

The natives wouldn't be enslaved, so most were hunted and killed. African slaves were brought to Bahia to help with the cultivation of new plants, mostly coffee, cotton, tobacco, sugar and cocoa.

In the 1700s a gold rush broke out in Minas Gerais. Most of the gold and precious stones were extracted (under strict supervision by the Portuguese crown) and sent to Europe for trading.

The locals didn't like the idea of not seeing the profits, so they started plotting independence from Portugal.

The capital of Brazil was moved from Salvador to Rio (not because of the night life).

In the middle of the 19th century, the British abolished slavery and forced other emerging economies to do the same, so no one would have a competitive advantage. Brazil followed suit and abolished slavery.

In the meantime, Brazil became a republic after the king of Portugal lost his throne to democracy.

In the 20th century, there was a massive influx of Germans, Italians and Japanese, which helped organize the place a bit.

Brazil was never in any major war, mostly because Brazilians don't really want to live anywhere else in the world.

Luckily, it was never attacked by anyone, except the French and the Dutch, who kept trying to invade the Northeast, but where repeatedly defeated.

Culture: The Candomblé Religion

Y ou can't take the jungle out the cat, and the portuguese couldn't take the African religion out of the slaves. So what happens when the master prohibits his slaves from practicing their religion, and forces them to practice his? Brazilian slaves realized that their African religion's rituals could be cloaked under Catholic rituals and symbolo- gy. What emerged is what is called sincretism: two religions paralleled by similar practice. In this case, Catholicism and Candomble.

(Gods/saints) were secretly being praised together with Catholic saints, so that the master would be under the impressions that they were properly converted, and hence less whipping.

At the same time, many rituals could not be performed in a church, due to their extravagance, so slaves created sites to practice various rites, usually hidden in the cane fields.

The Candomble religion, still practiced in present day Bahia, was always oppresed by the

Catholic society, which did not understand it, but was never extinguished. 30 Years ago, a law was passed recognizing the religion and all its rituals.

You can hire a tour guide to visit one of the night rituals. It is highly recommended that you behave during the ritual, wear white clothes and refrain from taking photos. What they are experiencing is meta-physical, way beyond your kung-fu skills. And the last thing you want is beef with the meta-physical.

Middah Borges
middahalegria@hotmail.com
9119-2155
R$300 for 2 persons

IF you want to see a show about the Candomble and Capoeira, check out Solar do Unhao's Buffet show.

Check the yearly events calendar for a list of the various Candomble festivities. (Most happen between December and January.)

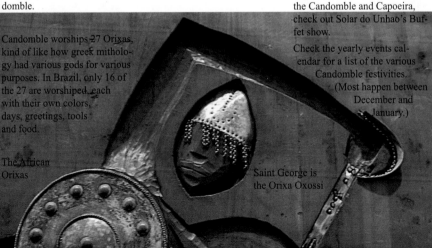

Candomble worships 27 Orixas, kind of like how greek mithology had various gods for various purposes. In Brazil, only 16 of the 27 are worshiped, each with their own colors, days, greetings, tools and food.

The African Orixas

Saint George is the Orixa Oxossi

Culture: Capoeira

Capoeira was an african fighting style that in Brazil developed into a dance and game. It started off in Angola under the name of "Zebra Game" and was imported together with a suitcase of African customs during colonial slavery.

Just like Candomble, it was oppressed by the slave masters and its practice forbidden. Slaves did not want to let go of this valuable and cultural art, so they kept practicing it se-cretely in clearings in the sugar cane fields. Since they did not want to leave any injuries on their partners, which would serve as evidence, they removed physical contact while mainting the moves and blows. It persisted, despite repeated oppression, police scuffles and manhunts for over 400 years.

In the 20th century, there were two men that made Capoeira a strong cultural phenomenon: Mater Pastinha and Master Bimba. The first, Pastinha, followed and taught the "Angolan Capoeira" style to students in the 1930s. This style is slower, closer to the ground and uncanny. It is also the fundamentals of Capoeira.

The second, Mestre Bimba, started promoting a new style, "Capoeira Regional" to black and white students in Salvador. This style is influenced by mar-tial arts, is more choreographed, has more jumps and saults, more leg work and if faster than the former.

Both styles have their own music and song, commonly played on a Berimbau, rhythmed by clap and chanted by those in the circle participating.

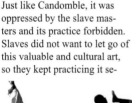

WHERE TO SEE IT
Associacao Capoeira Mestre Bimba, Tue-Fri 19h

Mercado Modelo, all week till 17h (bring change for contribution)

Federacao Brasileira de Capoeira Angola, Tue-Fri 19h

Pelourinho Attractions Map

1. St. Francisco Church
2. 3rd St. Francisco Order Church
3. St. Domingos Church
4. St. Pedro dos Cléricos Church
5. St. Salvador Cathedral
6. Eugênio Texeira Leal – Money´s Museum
7. Tereza Batista Show Square
8. Pedro Arcanio Show Square

9. Tempostal – Picture and Post Museum
10. Art – Culture – Memory Square
11. Abelardo Rodrigues Sacra Art Museum
12. Rosário dos Pretos Church
13. Benin Africa Culture House
14. Jorge Amado House Fundation

15. City Museum
16. Antropologic and Etnografic Museum
17. Quincas Berro D´água Show Square
18. African – Brazilian Museum
19. Abelardo Rodrigues Museum
20. Lacerda Elevator
21. Mercado Modelo

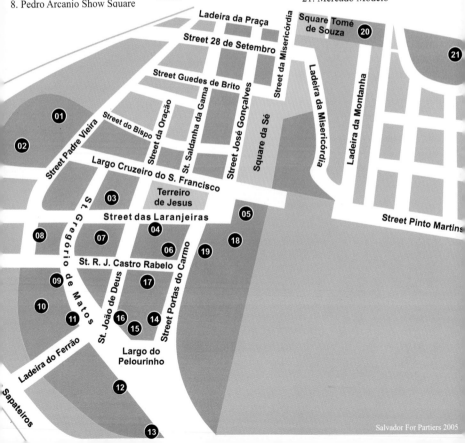

Salvador For Partiers 2005

Culture: Pelourinho Overview

Pelourinho can be safely experienced in 2 days and 2 nights. There you can find 22 museums, 13 church-es, 7 squares, dozens of restaurants and live shows. Est.Total Time (T): 8h Est.Total Cost (C): R$100 Best on: Sunny Weekday

Pelourinho and the historic cen-ter where the residential district to the upper class of Salvador up until 1855, when a cholera epídemic forced everyone to other neighbourhoods. Soon the property owners started rent-ing it very cheap to anyone, mostly hookers, drug addicts, crooks and anyone else who didn't mind the little hell it had become. This lasted till 1974, when a governmental project started investing in the His-toric center to recoup the area as a touristic attraction. It took 20 years before it was tourist friendly, and that made a world of a difference in establishing Salvador as Brazil's second des-tination.

Day 1

1 CATEDRAL BASILICA

This matre-cathedral was the first established by the Jesuits initially built between 1657 and 1672, but took over a hundred years to complete. Because of the slow rate at which it was decorated, it ended up having 5 different design styles: barroque, manerism, rococco, neo-classi-cal and renaissance roman.

2 IGREJA SÃO FRANCISCO

This is the city's main church attraction: a baroque/rococ-co church covered with 900kg (1900 Lbs) of gold. Why? Dur-ing the 18th century, while the economy was fervently prosper-ing from the land, the rich fami-lies wanted to show off a little, becaming the church for the up-per class.

3 ROSARIO DOS PRETOS CHURCH

A church built by the slaves, for the slaves. Although simple in decora-tions, its masses have better song, dance and rhythm than most. Be sure to check out their eclectic mass on Tuesdays at 6pm.

COFFEE

In between museums, a nice and relaxing stop for coffee in the many cafes. The hippest of them is BahiaCafe.com, also an in-ternet cafe. Also try their cocoa fruit juice (not chocolate).
BahiaCafe.com
Praca da Sé

4 LACERDA ELEVATOR

Today you'll ride and elava-tor! Whoop-tee-doo! No, really. It is a centu-ry old elevator that connect the lower city (busi-ness distric and docks) with the historic center. Not much to see, but better than walking up hill.

5 MERCADO MODELO

An old slave trading market that became a flew market after slavery was abolished. Now it's main attraction are the various stands selling all kinds of hand made souvenirers. Capoeira dancers can be watched in the back as they perform. Do donate something if you take photos.

Day 2

MUSEU DA ARTE SACRA (ABELARDO RODRIGUES)

Although 5 minutes from the historic center, this sacred art museum is a must to everyone one interested in Salvador's culture.

MUSEU AFRO-BRAZILEIRO

This Afro-Brazilian Museum has the largest col-lection of slave culture, both from Africa and of their own de-velopment in Brazil.

MUSEU DA CIDADE

The city museum that in one place shows a bit of everything Salvador is known for: food, music, history, slavery, coloniza-tion etc. If you can only see one museum, see this one.

STREET DRUMS

Just about everynightt there are various drum trouppes perform-ing their rhythm through the Pelourinho. Free.

MESTRE BIMBA CAPOEIRA

Want to see a real capoeira class? Check out Master Bimba's stu-dents sing and dance at 7pm every Tuesdays and Thursdays.

OLODUM SHOW

Brazil's most famous drum trouppe performs every Tuesday from 9pm to 12am. R$40 tix.

PERSONAL TOUR GUIDES

Contact Coconut Bahia for last minute tour guides
Coconut Bahia
Rua Gregório de Matos,06 Pelourinho
/322-1287
info@coconutbahia.com.br

Salvador For Partiers 2005

Cultural: City Tour

Before exploring Salvador`s various cultures and attractions, a day-long city tour will give you an overview of what the city has to offer. Estimate Total Time (T): 8h Estimated Total Cost (C): R$ 130 Best on: Sunny Weekday

Find a tour guide with a car that will fit all.

call the tour guide sindicate and order a guide.
Singtur

ICE-CREAM AT RIBEIRA

Every Salvadorian's favourite ice-cream parlour, due to it's large number of flavours and to its endurance over the years.

1 IGREJA BONFIM

Bonfim Church is a landmark, due to it's geographic location on a little peninsula in the bay, and due to its inumerous attenders. It is also the center of attraction during the month of January, when virtually everyone in the city comes over to wash it's stairs, making it into one of the world's largest public events.

Apart from a cool name, it has great view of the bay and the lower city. A 30 minute stop.

3 FEIRA SAO JOAQUIM

An extremely different, non-touristic attraction is to stop over at the fruit/produce/chicken fair and experience a real third-world market. A great place to buy and try all the fruits you never had.

4 SOLAR DO UNHAO

The Modern Art Museum, located in an old slave quarter, is nice quick stop for you to see

weird but cool artworks by Bahian artists.

5 VITORIA CORREDOR MUSEUMS

Along the Corredor da Vitoria there are three museums: the Carlos Costa Pinto, the Arqueology and the Bahian Art museum, each of which can be seen in under 20 minutes.

6 LATE LUNCH AT FAROL DA BARRA

The Barra Lighthouse is a must, not only because of its view in to the bay and out in the ocean, but because the maritime museum is located in it. The outdoor varanda is great place for photos, and it's cafe is not just a tourist attraction, it is actually tasty!

7 STROLL ALONG BARRA BEACH

Take off your shoes and digest it off with a nice stroll along the beach and back. Then drive or walk over to Morro de Cristo.

8 MORRO DE CRISTO

Not much to do, but that's the point: get a beer, sit on the grass between the palm trees and enjoy the view of sundown in Salvador. Leave once dark, before the mosquitos bite.

9 GIFT SHOPPING

Head over to Video Hobby Mega Store to check out the books and CDs from and about Brazil.
Video Hobby Mega Store
Av. Euclides da Cunha 22, Graça

OR CHECK EMAIL
Internet Cafe .Com
Porto da Barra

WHAT TO DO AT THE BEACH

READ THIS BOOK

During your first day at the beach, while you wait for a butt to pass by, read this book! It will guarantee you a great time.

FRESCOBOL

The paddle ball game the Brazilians play is one of the few non-competitive sports in the world. Stand 15ft (5m.) apart, close to the water, and paddle away.

BODY SURF

Body surfing is probably the purest water sport in the world. That means you can have fun with nature without any equipment, even swimming trunks. As a wave is passing you by, jump with it, do two strokes so your body catches up to the speed of the wave, and ride the wake.

BEER

Hey! Now we're talking! Beer drinking at the beach is everybody's favorite sport. But do drink some water every now and then, as you are probably dehydrating faster than you think, which will make you sleepy by dusk, ruining your nightlife.

JOG

Feel like exercising or sweating off yesterday's hangover? Jog along the beach. No further explaining needed…

BUTT-WATCH

Inevitable.

EAT CRAB

Why not, you got all day... and at R$3 a pop, it's worth it even if only for the ritual. Take your anger out on it with a mallet, rip it apart and eat any white meat you come across. Once done, go for a swim to watch yourself off.

What not to do

DON'T TRY THE SHRIMP FROM THE WALKING VENDORS

Certain death. Get it from the kiosks that make it on the spot.

DON'T MAKE EYE CONTACT WITH THE VENDORS

If you do, they will come and pester you for several minutes. When they catch your attention, quickly give them the no sign by shaking you index finger just twice.

GUYS: DON'T LIE DOWN ON THE SAND

That's for women or guys accompanied by their girl-friends.

DON'T FORGET TO TAKE OFF YOUR SUNGLASSES

Raccoon eyes are not cool in Salvador.

DON'T LEAVE YOUR STUFF UNGUARDED

When going into the water, simply ask your beach neighbor to watch your stuff for you. If you brought a digital camera or large amounts of money, one of your group should stay behind.

What to do in Pelourinho

Get a Bonfin Ribbon

Before you even remember, street kids will be offering you a Bonfim ribbon. If you don't have one, accept it and give him R$1. Two Reasons: 1) You can make 3 wishes as they tie it around your wrists. 2) They can never bother you again, as you already have one. Note: For the wishes to come true, the ribbon has to fall of naturally.

Jewelry Shop

Want a lesson in precious stones? Most of the jewellers can teach you the basics of the various Brazilian stones, how they are found, cut, designed, graded and their financial values in Brazil and their appreciation abroad.

Lauritano Jewels
Rua das Laranjeiras 52, Pelourinho

Get Blessed

Look for this man. He may not be a priest of any kind, but he will read your palm, take a small branch spank you while saying a prayer to bless you soul. Can't hurt.

Acaraje

You can have an acaraje any-wher in the city, but it really make more sense in Pelourinho. Kind of like beer to pubs, hot-dog to stadiums and martinis to lounges.

Cravinho

A cachaca based drink aged in oak barrels with various ingredients. One or two are fine, more will get to your head without you knowing, which can be desireable.

Fallen Cross Chilling

The fallen cross is a monument made to protest the removal of a church to make room for tram tracks. Although a one-liner, the view from the place is beautiful enough to deserve a beer/wine/soda.

Photo-op with the Baiana

You can either hug and kiss the Bahiana (cheek), or you can wear the hat and stand behind the prop. Makes great photos.

Hair Braiding

You should look silly at least once in your life, so why not here? You can get your hair braided dirt cheap at Terreiro de Jesus.

BEACH OPTIONS

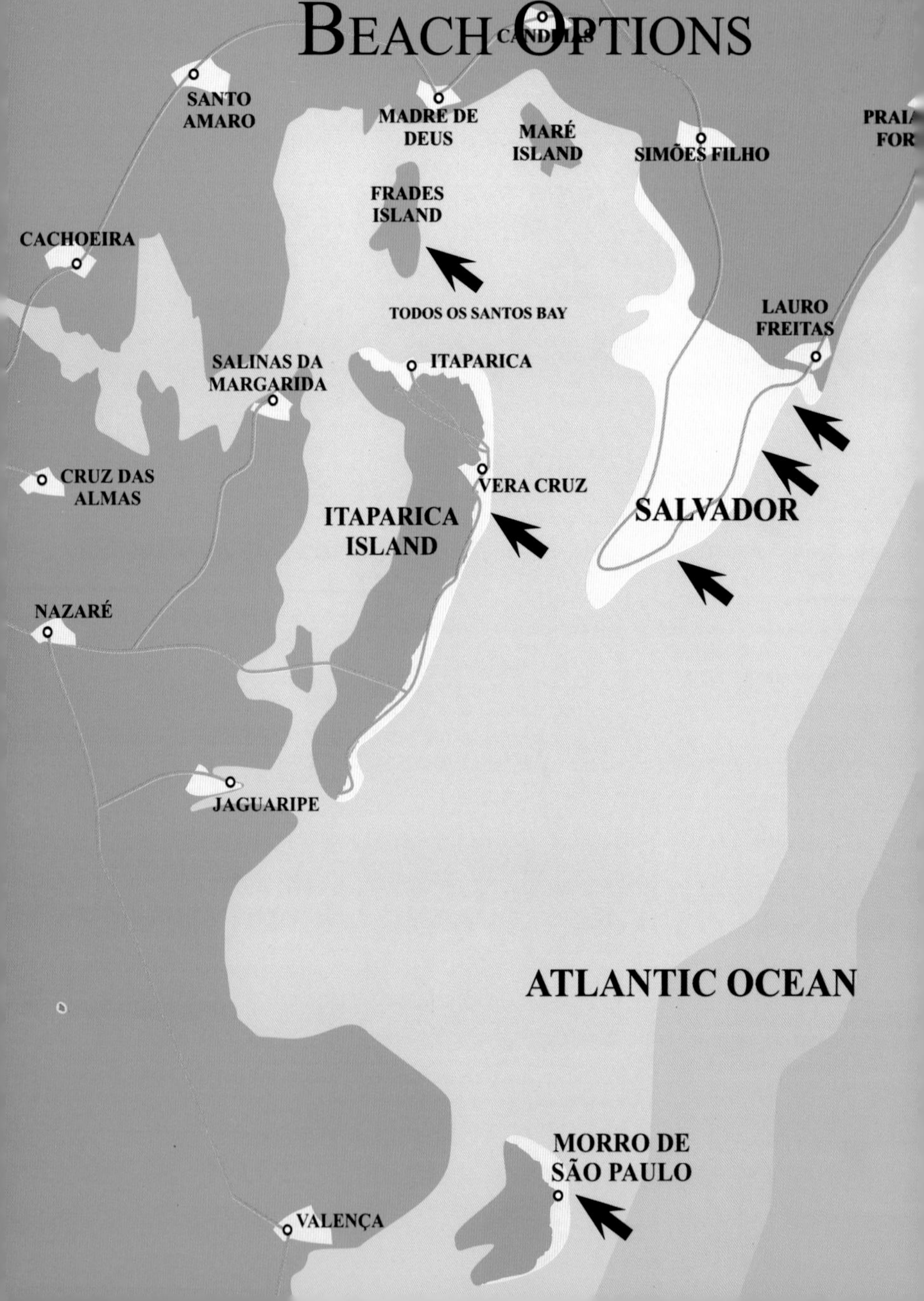

CANDEIAS

SANTO
AMARO

MADRE DE
DEUS

MARÉ
ISLAND

SIMÕES FILHO

PRAIA
FOR

FRADES
ISLAND

CACHOEIRA

LAURO
FREITAS

TODOS OS SANTOS BAY

SALINAS DA
MARGARIDA

ITAPARICA

CRUZ DAS
ALMAS

VERA CRUZ

SALVADOR

ITAPARICA
ISLAND

NAZARÉ

JAGUARIPE

ATLANTIC OCEAN

MORRO DE
SÃO PAULO

VALENÇA

Relax: City Beach-Hopping

ou've just arrived and you want to unwind before expliring Salvador's culture. Hop on a cab and head
a few beaches, spending an hour or two at each. Estimate Total Time (T): 8h Estimated Total Cost (C): R$ 130   Best
: Sunny Weekday

As a general, the further north you go ,the better the eaches get. The best way to xperience Salvador's beaches is start off with the ones close to arra, and hop over to the next ne north, thus having an always nproved experience.

JUICE AT SUCOS 24HR

ven if you had reakfast, a tropical uit juice will help et your nutrients to healthy level, plus ey taste great

) JAGUARIBE BEACH

great beach any day of the eek.

PIATA

urfer beach

) LUNCH AT FLAMENGO BEACH

eafood at any of the beach ki-sks usually involve lobsters, nrimp, crab, rice, salad and ther side dishes, all for a mea-

sly sum of R$60 or less, where 4 can eat.

5) BEER AND ACARAJE AT ITAPOAN

Considered by most Brazilian the most relaxing place in the country (it`s not), due to a fa-mous bossanova song that talks about spending an afternoon there. Kind of like Hotel Cali-fornia. Do make sure to try the world`s best Acaraje: Cira`s. Ask anyone in Salvador and they know.

Relax: Praia do Forte Village

Its cute, its safe and it has lots to do. Two days is the bare minimum to start discovering this fisherman village, now home to Brazil`s largest sea-turtle sanctuary.

(C): R$ 60   Best on: Cloudy Weekday

Hop on a bus or rent a car and head over to Praia do Forte, 80 minutes north of Salvador.

Stuff to do:

BEACH

The better beaches are north or south of the village.

QUADRICYCLE *

They have 90 minute tours of the forest, the dunes or the beaches, all on these dune bikes. Fun for the kids or drunk adults (joke).

FOREST RESERVE

A great 2 hour tour of a Brazilian Atlantic forest, with various exotic fruits and animals loose.

TAMAR TURTLE SANCTUARY

Brazil`s largest sea-turtle sanctuary. Sea turtles bigger than coffee tables. Their gift shop has amazingly well designed souveniers.
www.projetotamar.org

D`AVILA CASTLE

One Brazil`s largest and most coveted castles, home to the one the largest and richest families during colonial times.

DIVING *

Take diving lessons, or at least go through a baptism and enjoy the coral life unspoiled in this part of the country. Warm clear waters.

WHALE WATCHING *

Yes, just like tourists every winter they come to this area looking for warm waters to have sex err, mate.

NATURAL POOLS

There are dozens of natural pools spread along the coast of Praia do Forte. Instead of sitting on the sand, break tradition and sit in one of these all day.

* Odara Tours Agency
(071) 676 1080
www.odaratours.com.br

UNE-BUGGY
IDES *

he have trips to
e dunes in vari-
us forms: buggy,
uadricycle, horse
c. All of them fun.

MBASSAI *

true paradise on Earth, 20
inutes north of the village.
ook for buses heading that
ay.

WHERE TO EAT

ny of the various restaurants
the main street in the village
e sure shots. If you want an
xtremely cheap seafood plat-
r, shoot for Canteiro do Pi-
ta, where 2 can eat a seafood
latter for under R$40.

anteiro do Pirata
raça dos Artistas, P. do Forte
0% discount with this book

WHERE TO STAY

raia do Forte Hostel
ww.albergue.com.br

ousada Ogum Marinho
ww.ogummarinho.com.br -

ousada Sobrado da Vila
ww.sobradodavila.com.br
ww.viladoscorais.com.br

NIGHTLIFE

ts has a quiet nightlife during
ow-season (bars and restau-
ants), but bumps during high
eason (Jan- March). Given its
small village, all parties are
asy to find.

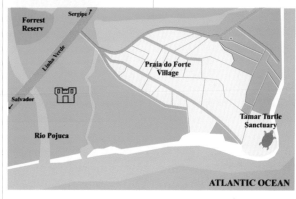

Forrest Reserv

Sergipe

Linha Verde

Salvador

Rio Pojuca

Praia do Forte Village

Tamar Turtle Sanctuary

ATLANTIC OCEAN

Relax: Morro de São Paulo Island

Morro de Sao Paulo is a get-away village in the paradise island of Tinhare, deserving at least 2 days. It is 100km south of Salvador so you`ll need to spend the night. During the summer Brazilians from around the country take over and turn the place into a party town.

GET THERE

Either take the:

• Catamaran (from the Porto Maritimo, next to the Mercado Modelo, R$45 each way) or

• The aero-taxi (small propelor plane departing from the airport, R$180 each way).

WHERE TO STAY

There are dozens of pousadas (inns) in MSP. We liked this one:
Pousada Farol do Morro
www.faroldomorro.com.br

Tours

After plunking down your bags an putting on your skimp swimwear, hire a tour guide (usually found in the docks) and ask for the mud and forest tour. Most don`t speak english, but they can guide you through the trails like anyone else.

PINK MEDICINAL MUD

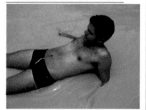

Ever want to wallow like a pig, and look ridiculous Of course you do. And here you can do it for free on the pink clay streams leading to the beach. Cover yourself and then walk around like a zombie till it dries. Your skin will thank you for it.

FONTE DO CEU WATERFALL

Although it`s no Niagara, it is conveniently located in the middle of your jungle trekking, just when the clay will have dried. Wash yourself off in the warm water.

FORTE TAPIRANDU

The ruins of a fort protecting the island from the dutch and french.

LIGHTHOUSE

Great views of the island all around

AIRCABLE

Slide down Brazil`s tallest aircable, scary as hell but you`d be nuts not do it. Afterwards you`ll want to do it over and over, if it weren`t for the steep price of R$20 per ride.

PASTELARIA NATIVO

Go for a huge shrimp pastel (camarao) at the kiosk at the end of beach 2.

Beaches

hey are all great, none are dirty, ut each can appeal to your ood: Beach 1 is filled with ki-sks, ideal for beers. Beach 2 s the younger beach, with vol-yball courts and surfer dudes. each 3 has little room for ly-ng down, but ideal for a horse ack ride. Beach 4 has natural ools and beach 5, Enchantment each, is the more secluded of hese 5, but no hanky-panky!

Activities

SCUBA DIVING

io for a baptism or lessons if you are staying longer) as here are crystal clear corals and ools all over the island, filled vith sea life (not just stupid sea veed).

ISLAND JEEP TOUR

A 60 minute tour of the island, vhere you can see different veg-tation, beaches and wild-life.

HORSE-BACK RIDING

Rent the horse for an hour or two at most, as your city-slick-ing ass will hurt.

PLANA-SUB

The coolest water sport invented in Brazil: put your snorkel on and let a boat tug you through the coral reefs and seaworld. The board can be used to take you down, up, left or right, just like Nintendo. You`ll want to do this again and again, and it`s worth it!

BOIPEBA ISLAND

The beautiful island south of Tinhare is quieter, more relaxed and under developed just enough to attract the "I want to get away" crowd.

Dinner

From our survey, these restau-rants came out on top:
Sabor da Terra
Tinhare
Kiosk St. Luzia
La Onda
Pizza Forno a Lenha

Nightlife
BEACH BARS

In Beach 2. Jamaica Bar and 89 are everyone`s favourites, but the fruit cocktails served outside shouldn`t be skipped.

"BEACH 2" LUAUS

Just about every day during high season.

TOCA DO MORCEGO

A party shack up close to the Lighthouse, where no matter what they play, everyone dances.

SKINNY DIPPING

In the hidden beaches (beach 1, 3, 4 or 5)

Relax: Schooner trip

Schooner trips are great since they are not about the destination but about the trip themselves.

Est.Total Time (T): 8h Est. Total Cost (C): R$ 50   Best on: Sunny Weekday

The schooner leaves at 9am from the Porto Maritimo heading for Itaparica Island, stopping at a beach around 11am, then heading to Frade Island at 1pm, arriving back in Salvador at 5pm. This means you`ll have to wake up early and be sober to avoid sea-sickness. We recommend having lunch at the second island, so you may just sleep on your way back to Salvador.

The best way to guarantee a great schooner trip is 1) to make sure you go on a sunny day 2) to make sure you go with a group of friends and 3) to make sure everyone starts drinking early. If you are not with a group of friends, you should start organizing a trip with people you meet in Salvador: from your hotel, from the nightlife and other tours you did. It´s guar-

anteed boredom if you go on a boat filled with unacquainted couples.

Before boarding, you should pass by a supermarket and buy junk food for everyone.

Most schooners sell drinks at affordable rates, so open a tab and start pounding. If its just you and your friends on the schooner, you can make it "all-inlcusive" and have an open bar for

R$20 to R$30 a head. That`ll get people drinking faster.

And since this is a party boat, there`s gotta be music. Bring your favourite CDs, as long as its upbeat and gets people dancing. Don`t let anyone sit down during the trip.

MS Turismo
contact: Geraldo
Centro Maritimo, Comercio
319-3431 or 9151-8147
R$25 pp with this guide (reg. R$30)

Relax: Speed Boat Tour

ant to check out all the various islands around Salvador in style? A speed boat will get you around to
l the attractions, like Morro de Sao Paulo, Valenca, Boipeba, Itaparica and Frades island.

ou have 2 choices: a five hour
ur or a 2 day tour (or more).
Vith that decided, you can then
noose the right type of speed
oat for your tour.

HOUR TRIP

going for the 5 hour tour,
our best bet is to cruise around
1e bay, stopping at the various
eaches on Taparica and Frades
land. Crystal clear waters,
1lm beaches (on weekdays)
ith great seafood at most ki-
sks (mostly grilled fish, shrimp
r lobster). As is expected, ask
1e rental company to fill up the
idge with party supplies and
1nk food.

WO DAY TRIP

going for the 2 or more days
ur of the region, the recom-
1ended tour is do the bay in one

day and sleep in the boat or in an
inn in Taparica. Inns aren`t hard
to find.

Next day head to Morro de Sao
Paulo (which is a 60km south of
the bay), an hour`s trip. There
you can see all the attractions,
party and sleep there.

Next day, hop over to Boipeba,
which is even more relaxed than
the last two, as it is less touristic. At the end of the day, tell the

captain to head back to Salvador with a "Captain, set course
for Salvador....we`re heading
home!" Arms behind your back
and stare at the horizon.

Doug Simon Boat Rentals
dsimonbr@yahoo.com
9132-9155
www.bahiaproperty.com
5 hour trip:
- **28ft Speed boat rental with captain,
fits 4 to 6 = R$500**
- **Cabin Cruiser, 38ft speed boat with
captain fits 12 = R$1050/day**
Two day tour:
- **Cabin Cruiser, 38ft speed boat with
captain, sleeps 6 to 8 = R$1450/day**
Party supplies not included.

If you want a sail boat, these
guys can hook you up.
MS Turismo
contact: Geraldo
Centro Maritimo, Comercio
319-3431 or 9151-8147
call for prices

What to do in Salvador

Massage Parlor

You can also get a massage (a real massage, not sex) at several massage parlors. The rates range from $35 to $80 an hour. Most of them specialize in Shiatsu-style massage, a deep muscle massage. Most have accupuntur too, doesn't hurt.
Shopping da Barra

Happy Hours

Another option for tourists from cold climates is to enjoy the fact that it is raining yet hot. To best observe this, we recommend drinking along with your rain watching. Great places to do all this are at:

Cruz do Pascoal (ocean view)
Rua Joaquim Tavora, St. Antonio

Barra Vento (ocean view)
Barra

Casa Amarela
Rua das Hortencias 288, Pituba

To Nem Ai
Rua das Hortencias 246, Pituba

Bar da Ponta (ocean view)
Avenida Contorno

Pietro's Bar (ocean view)
Rua Rio Negro 6, Mont Serrat

Capoeira Lessons

You can either sit around waiting for the sun to come out, or you can go learn a few capoeira moves! Really! There are two capoeira schools you can call up any time and schedule private lessons (individual or group).

Give them an hour to get the instructors ready, and head over there.

Mestre Bimba
Rua das Laranjeiras, Pelourinho
322 0639

Scuba Lessons

Hey! It is raining! Why not get wet? Go get some scuba diving lessons!
See page 32 for details.

WHEN IT'S RAINING

FRUIT TASTING AT THE PRODUCE FAIR

Head over to Feira S. Joaquim with R$20 in small bills and try all the exotic fruits you can find.
Check page ?? for fruits.

MALL

Heck, you are bound to find a lot of the same international shops at the local malls (Levi's, Armani, etc.) but some shops offer stuff at good prices you can't find elsewhere: Brazilian pants for women (the ones that go up your butt), shoes and bags, beach gear.
Check page ?? for gift ideas and a list of recommended malls.

BEAUTY CLINIC

Ladies: Hair cuts, facials, nails etc. are all so cheap in Brazil, that they are worth it whether it is raining or not.

You can go to one these place and get the works (hair, nails, waxing, facial, massage etc.) for under R$200.
See page 72

MUSEUMS

The museums listed on page ?? may offer enough content to last a few hours without boring you to death.

SMOKE A CIGAR

Heck, it takes 3 hours to go through one. If you have never smoke but want to try, just calmly puff till the nicotine starts to sink in, usually within 15 minutes
BahiaCafe.com
Praca da Se, Centro Historico

BRAZILIAN JEWEL TOUR

Brazil has the largest variety of precious and semi-precious stones, which helped speed up Brazil's colonization. Most shops offer a free tour of the stone mining, jewel designing and handcrafting process. If you are into buying, Lauritano Jewel shop has some of the best prices, since they own the emerald mines, cutting out middle men.
Lauritano Jewels
Rua das Laranjeiras 52

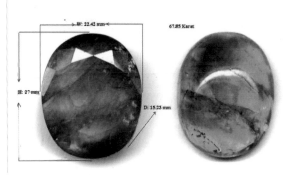

Sports: Scuba Diving

If you ever wanted to learn to scuba dive, this is it. You can take a day course called a "baptism", which you spend an hour learning the theory, then get into the water with an instructor by your side.

This baptism won't get you certified (which allows you to rent equipment and go off on your own) but will count towards certification. Dive Bahia offers the baptism in a variety of warm water reefs.

Dive Bahia
Contact: Marcos
264-3820
Porto da Barra 3809, Barra
www.divebahia.com.br
divebahia@divebahia.com.br

R$153 (reg. R$170) pp, quick course plus 45 minute guided dive

FULL-COURSE

If you would like to get certified, you can take a full scuba course, which takes a few days. **R$540 (reg R$600)**

GEAR RENTAL

You can also rent equipment from them, should you have your certification ready.
R$160, gear + 2 cylinder, boar and sailor

Sports: Kite-surfing

Kite surfing is the coolest shit! It is the newest water sport and is something you can learn during your stay in Salvador. Not only is Salvador a great place to practice and learn the sport, but down here lessons are also very affordable compared to 1st World prices (usually about 1/5 of what a similar course runs for out there).

However, it is not for every one. You have to be in shape. If you haven't been working out, you won't be able to keep up with the four-hours-a-day lessons.

They are very demanding. Sort of like working out at the gym for 4 hours.

The fastest way to learn it is to take a 2-day class. The first day you learn how to fly the kite and then to body-drag, which is to lay in the water and control the kite so it drags you around. The next day you learn to stand up on the board, and possibly do a few maneuvers and jumps.

There are two places in Salvador where the sport can be practiced: Praia de Buraquinho, 30 km north of the city where a river merges with the ocean, offering flat waters, ideal for beginners. The second place is Praia da Terceira ponte, close to Rio Vermelho, with constant on-shore wind and waves for saults.

Patrick Goncalves
www.patrickgoncalves.com
9141-9090 / 285-4888
kite@patrickgoncalves.com
equipment included, english speaking instructors
2 day course (8 hours): R$450 (regular R$540)
4 day course (16 hours): R$720

Sports: Surfing

Surfing is still the coolest beach sport. Just mentioning it impresses the ladies anywhere in the world. But learning it is hard, exhausting, and takes many days. From the two hours you spend in the water, over 60 minutes are spent swimming on the board. The other 55 are spent waiting for a wave, and the last 2 minutes is the time you spend riding the wave. (Really, no shit).

Unless you are staying more than a week in Salvador, we don't recommend taking the classes as they will take up 2 hours a day and wear you out for the rest of the day. Unless you are in Olympic conditions, you won't be able to take more than 2 hours a day.

Most students are only able to stand on the board on the second day, and it takes about 7 lessons before you are doing basic maneuvers. But, if you have started taking lessons elsewhere,

feel confident about your physical condition and want to try it anyway, we recommend this professional surf academy:

AcaSurf Surf School
Contact: Jose Augusto
www.acasurf.com.br
367-0948 or 9192-1616
acasurf@ig.com.br
equipment included, english and spanish speaking instructors. Classes take place in Jaguaribe beach.

R$45/hour/person (R$50 regular) discounts for larger groups
Transfer not included.

Sports: Bodyboarding

A more realistic alternative to learning to surf is to body-board. It is much easier to learn (you pick up the basic moves in under an hour), less tiring, and you ride the waves longer. All these are arguments in favor of this sport. It loses to surfing only in that surfing has a stable status. At the same time, many argue that bodyboarding is a radical version of surf, while safer.

Riding a wave on a bodyboard is idiotically simple, but instructors can teach you the cool stuff: back flips, rolls, 360 and an endless sea of tribal jargon. Plus, you learn to ride big waves at high speeds. We recommend these guys:

AcaSurf Surf School
Contact: Jose Augusto
www.acasurf.com.br

367-0948 or 9192-1616
acasurf@ig.com.br
equipment included, english and spanish speaking instructors

R$45/hour/person (R$50 regular) discounts for larger groups
Transfer not included.

BRAZILIAN

Brazilian traditional cuisine uses a wide variety of readily-available ingredients. But most are cooked with simple culinary techniques: boil it or fry it. This makes the different dishes seem almost rudimentary and very 18th Century. At the same time, most of the ingredients are rich in flavor, and therefore do not need complicated culinary improvement.

BAHIAN FOOD

Muqueca (Seafood stew)

Vatapa (fish piree)

Bahian food is where Brazilian ingredients meet African recipes. Coconut milk, palm oil, black eye peas, okra, cassava and thank God: seafood. Most take the form of a stew or puree: Muqueca de Camarao (Shrimp stew in coconut sauce), Bobo de Camarao (Shrimp again) and Vatapa .

Yemanjá
Av. Otávio Mangabeira , 4655
Jardim Armação
(71) 461-9010 / (71) 461-9008

SENAC
Largo do Pelourinho , 13 / 19 , 2nd floor,
Pelourinho
(71) 321-5502

Sorriso da Dadá
Rua Frei Vicente 5, Pelourinho
(71) 321-9642

CHURRASCO

Picanha (Top Sirloin)

Aipim (Cassava)

Churrasco is an Argentinian style barbecue of different cuts of meat. With the exception of salt, the meats are cooked with no spices or sauces, because the chef wants to show his guests that the quality and flavor of the meat does not need to be camouflaged. A Churrascaria serves endless rounds of meats on an all-you-can-eat price basis, with drinks and deserts served sepa-

rately. Good for more relaxed nights, as binge eating will slow you down on the dance floor.

Boi Preto
Av. Otávio Mangabeira , s/n
Jardim Armação
(71) 362-8844

Barbacoa
Av. Tancredo Neves , 909
(71) 342-4666

Sal e Brasa
Rua Carimbamba 917, Pituaçu
(71) 461-1999

Rincão Gaúcho
Rua Pedro Silva Ribeiro 429, Jardim
Armação
(71) 461-4035

FEIJOADA

Feijoard (bean stew)

CUISINES

The three most traditional dishes, "Feijoada", "Bacalhoada" and "Tutu à Mineira" were all "slave" foods: rich in carbohydrades, proteins and fat, all needed to compensate for excessive manual labor. Due to their rich flavor, they were eventually adopted by all social classes.

Couve&Aipim (kale&cassava)

Probably the most typical dish from Brazil: a black bean stew with hearty sausages, sun-dried beef, served with rice, couve, cassava flour and orange. This will also slow you down on the dance floor.

HEALTH

Prato de Verao (fruit dish)

It is hard to find nighttime healthy-food restaurants, as most Locals would rather eat healthy during the day.

Ramma
Rua Lorde Cochrane 76, Barra Avenida
(71) 264-0044

Manjericão
Rua Fonte do Boi 3b, Rio Vermelho
(71) 355-5641

Saúde na Panela
Rua das Hortênsias 752, Pituba
(71) 353-6788 / (71) 353-8088

PORTUGUESE

Bacalhau Portuguese (cod)

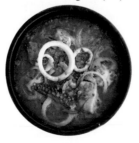

Bacalhoada Espanha (cod stew)

If you are not planning on going to Portugal in the near future, try their cuisine here! Given all the ingredients the Portuguese had access to in the last 800 years,

they use just about everything you can imagine.

Bacalhau do Martelo
Rua Doutor Odilon Santos , 205
Rio Vermelho
(71) 334-0458
www.bacalhaudemartelo.com.br

SEAFOOD

Camarao na Moranga (pumpkin shrimp)

Filet de Badejo (Seabass fillet)

There are 3 sea-food recipes that I urge gringos to try: the Bacalhoada (cod fish stew, developed by the sailors during colonial voyages), the Cavaquinha (slip-

BRAZILIAN

per lobster, with the tastiest tails in the world) and the grilled fish wrapped in banana leaves.

Solar do Unhao
An old slave quarter with a great seafood buffet. Includes an African-roots show (Candomble and Capoeira) that always wows visitors. Ask your concierge for tickets.
Av. Contorno s/n° - Comércio
329-5551or 329-5331

O Lagostão
Rua Professor Souza Brito , 12
Farol de Itapoá
(71) 375-3646

Maria Mata Mouro
Rua Inácio Accioli , 8
Pelourinho
(71) 321-3929

Mistura Fina
Rua Professor Souza Brito , 41
Farol de Itapoã
(71) 375-2623

Mamma Bahia
Pelourinho

CONTEMPORARY

The contemporary-cuisine chefs in Brazil are making an impressive rediscovery of local ingredients, by adding new twists to old recipes, or inventing altogether new dishes. If you want to taste the new wave in culinary talent, then these chefs will blown your taste buds away.

Salvador Pub
Rua do Meio 154, Rio Vermelho

Paraíso Tropical
Rua Edgar Loureiro , 98-b, Cabula
(71) 381-7464

Galpão
Av. do Contorno , 660
Comércio
266-5544

Trapiche Adelaide
Av.do Contorno
Comercio

Bar da Ponta
Av. do Contorno, Comercio

Pereira
Av. 7 de Setembro , 3959
Porto da Barra
(71) 264-6464

CUISINES (CONTINUED)

Soho
Rua Lafayete Coutinho , 1010
Comércio
(71) 322-4554 / (71) 322-5616

PIZZA

Brazilian pizza is a must: They are paper thin, wood-oven baked, and come in flavors Florence with it had.

Companhia da Pizza
Praça Brigadeiro Faria Rocha , s/n
Rio Vermelho
334-6276

Il Forno
Rua Alm. Marques Leao 77, Barra
264-7287

NORTHEASTERN

Aipim com carne seca (cassava with sun dried beef)

Northeaster food has sun dried beef at the center of attention and cassava as the main source of carbs, as this was what was appropriate, given the heat and lack of vegetation in Brazil's dry lands.

Gibão de Couro
Rua Mato Grosso 53, Pituba
(71) 240-6611

O Picuí
Rua Melvin Jones 91, Jardim Armação
(71) 461-9000

A Porteira
Rua Dom Eugênio Sales 96, Boca do Rio
(71) 461-3105 / (71) 461-3328

COMIDA A KILO/BUFFET

Prato Feito (daily dish of rice, beans, salad and steak)

Food by the pound. You pile your plate from the buffet, weight it, and pay on weight. Prices range from $10 to $28 per kilo.

Mignon Place
Rua Amélia Rodrigues 2, Graça
(71) 247-5774

Panorâmico
Rua das Laranjeiras 18 / 20, Pelourinho
(71) 321-2243

Coliseu Bar e Restaurante
Rua Cruzeiro do São Francisco 9 and 13,
Pelourinho
(71) 321-6918 / (71) 321-5585

Rabune Grill
Avenida Centenário 2992, Shopping
Barra / 1st Floor
(71) 267-2811

Musical Genre: Drum Troupes

The human psychological fasination with the drum is that it can change the pace of our heartsbeats. The faster and louder the more it accelerates and the more fervently emotional we get, hence the drum band in the military, in rituals and sacrifices and in rock. Bahia`s drum troupes make an orchestra out of drums, in probably the most powerful spectacles or sound one may ever come across.

WHERE TO HEAR IT LIVE:

Pelourinho

Wet&Wild (Sundays)

CDS AND BANDS TO LOOK FOR:

Olodum

Timbalada

Araketu

Musical Genre: Pagode

An improvised slower samba, made by beating anything that can be found at a bar table: spoon to a bottle as the cymbol, a chair as the drum, matchbox as the shaker etc. Dirty lyrics. Usually a woman starts to samba along to it. Great for afternoons and barbecues.

WHERE TO HEAR IT LIVE:

Beco da Gal (Wed)

Tropicana (Thu)

Viola Vadia (Fri)

CDS AND BANDS TO LOOK FOR:

Jorge Aragão

Zeca Pagodinho

Fundo De Quintal

Beth Carvalho

Musical Genre: Axé

Imagine music made for aerobics, without the 1 2 3 4. Axe mixes upbeat lyrics with upbeat melodies to get the crowd to move in sync. Right fist to the left, left fist to the right, squat down, turn etc. It`s ideal for day-time beach parties and shows, since you can always run and cool off in the water. During carnival and off-carnival parties, the bands perform on their supped-up trucks, driving through neighbourhoods.

CDS AND BANDS TO LOOK FOR:

Ivete Sangalo

Chiclete com Banana

Asa de Aguia

WHERE TO HEAR IT LIVE:

Carnival & Bigger festivals

Beach shows

Musical Genre: Funk

Nothing like American funk, but basically a retard on an electronic piano making noise after only one lesson. Mix that with dirty lyrics and what do you get? The biggest music craze in Brazil since the Lambada. Girls love dancing to it, guys love singing the naughty lyrics, parents hate it, in other words, just the way teenage music should be.

Some of the most famous are "I'll throw you on the bed and give lots of pressure" and "the horsy and the donkey took my mare for a walk, clopty clop, clopty clop, clopty clop". Regardless of whether the music makes your ears bleed, the women that listen to this are 90% *poposudas*, meaning, worth the sacrifice.

CDS AND BANDS TO LOOK FOR:

Mr Catra

Dj Marlboro

Cindinho E Doca

WHERE TO HEAR IT LIVE:

Wherever there is a crowd.

Musical Genre: Brazil Pop (MPB)

Caetano, Gil, Marisa Monte, Djavan and Jorge Benjor, amongst many others, used to play in the 60s and 70s a smooth and an upbeat Brazilian version of pop. Unfortunately, most of them offer poetic lyrics that don't mean anything when translated, making its enjoyment hard. But the instrumentals, melodies and voices are sufficient to please your ears. Get a Jorge Benjor for your car, Djavan for your sofa, Gil for your garden and Marisa Monte for your bed. If you make a Brazilian friend who is willing to translate, get Chico Buarque, and get ready for a major head-rush.

CDs AND BANDS TO LOOK FOR:

Gilberto Gil

Jorge Benjor

Caetano Veloso

Djavan

WHERE TO HEAR IT LIVE:

Pedra da Sereia

Bohemia

Emporio

Mariposa

Sesi

Musical Genre: Samba

The most famous Brazilian music, mostly of percussion and ukelete guitars. Very hard to stay still to. Ask someone to teach you the dance moves, as they seem hard, but are even harder when you try it. Can be heard at any of the samba school rehearsals. Goes great with beer or more hyper stuff.

WHERE TO HEAR IT LIVE:

Beco da Gal (Wed)

Tropicana (Thu)

Viola Vadia (Fri)

CDs AND BANDS TO LOOK FOR:

Sambas De Enredo Carnaval De 2004

Cartola

Jamelão

Casa De Samba (Coletânea)

Musical Genre: Forró

Forró music is a slowed-down version of the barn dance: very country. It was so out of style that it came back and is now popular again. Basically, you grab a girl (a great reason to grab women) and dance like everyone else in the room: real close rotating clockwise. Two steps out, Two steps in, then the other foot. Repeat all night.

CDs AND BANDS TO LOOK FOR:

Luis Gonzaga

Dominginhos

Jackson Do Pandeiro

WHERE TO HEAR IT LIVE:

Emporio (Weekends)

Lingua de Prata (Mon)

Musical Genre: Arrocha

No one thought music could get worse than Brazilian funk, but the musical genious in every Bahian made it possible. Picture a Casio keyboard built-in rhythm, the same riff repeated all night (the same melody for all the songs!) and lyrics only about anal sex! The first 6 times you hear it you`ll get ulcers from the cheesy music and corny dance. On the 7th, however, it`ll all change. You`ll be familiar with the (easy to memorize) music and your self-respect will make way for your desire to dance stupid. Thank God! And you`ll be liberated from any decent up-bringing your parents tried to offer you. You`ll shake it to the left, to the right, do a little turn and air-fuck till the sunrises.

Famous lyrics include "Gonna do you, gonna do you" and " In the front in the back..."

WHERE TO HEAR IT LIVE:

Ribeira or anywhere where there is a crowd.

YEARLY

JANUARY

VACATION MONTH

January is vacation month for schools and government offices. There are a dozen feasts between December and January, so find one won't be hard.

BONFIM CHURCH FEAST

Second Thursday in January everyone walks from downtown to Bonfim church to wash its stairs.

FEBRUARY

IEMANJA FEAST

Candomble religious feast offering gifts to the ocean Goddess. Feb 5th.

CARNIVAL*

Carnival is also the largest party of the year: 165 million people partying for a week. If you are here during carnival, be sure to get buy an "abada" to participate in any of the various trio-eletricos.

MARCH

PRESENTE DE YEMANJÁ DE HUMAITÁ

Candomble feast in Mont Serrat on the 8th of March.

RAMOS PROCESSION

Religious event around the 3rd week.

JULY

INDEPENDANCE FEAST

Another reason to party. July 2nd.

Mid-year school vacation month. Get-away destinations packed.

AUGUST

SAINT ROQUE FEST

16th Aug.

SEPTEMBER

COSME AND DAMIAN DAY

Kids get free candy. 27th Sept.

* LOOK FOR OUR CARNIVAL GUIDE AT
WWW.SALVADORFORPARTIERS.COM/CARNAVAL/

EVENTS

APRIL

HOLY WEEK

Various manifestations though-out the city, inclucing the Passion of Christ play in Dique do Tororo.

MAY

SAINT FRANCIS XAVIER PROCESSIONS

Another religious events that ends up transforming into a big party.

JUNE

Festa Junina

Festa Junina is hick fest. Everyone dresses like a hick and goes square dancing, Brazilian style of course. Usually these events are held between large groups of friends (100 or more), but some are run by a party promotion company. Worth a visit.

OCTOBER

CHILDREN'S DAY

An indirect reason to party.

NOVEMBER

BAIANA DAY

They deserve it, for making awesome acarajes at affordable prices. 25th Nov.

BLACK CONCIOUSNESS DAY

Gets everyone out on the street to drink and party. 6th Nov.

DECEMBER

FISHERMEN'S FEAST

Iemanja style feast. 2-5th Dec.

CONCEICAO DA PRAIA

Religious event turned party on December 8th.

NEW YEARS

Choose a club with an ocean view and go there.

PARTY & NIGHT OPTIONS

SALVADOR NIGHTLIFE

Live music is so common in Salvador you may have 17 options on a Monday night. There is no alcohol curfew, so bars and clubs close as soon as the house starts to empty.

CLUBS

The club scene is Salvador is limited to a few clubs, since most of the city would rather spend their money on 5 beer cans instead of one gin&tonic. The clubs found in this guide are usually frequented by Salvador's elite, whether they are 20 or 35 years old. Clubs tend to be for the single crowd, where they go to not be single for that night. Most clubs have live bands perform, so DJs are restricted to clubs like Fashion Club, Korunn and Satelite.

STREET PARTIES

It doesn't take much for a small get together to become a major street party. All you need is a beer vendor and car supped up with speakers in the back. You'll find a younger crowd at most of these places. These are a great option if you want to talk to other Brazilians. And these events are easy on your wallet, as there is never any entrance charge and beers aren't marked up.

LIVE MUSIC

Since Bahia invented Samba, MPB, Axe, Capoeira music, Batucadas and Arrocha, and since every Bahian heart beats to a rhythm, there is live music everywhere.

We've listed the places with Brazilian music being performed by local musicians. No international pop or big concerts found here.

CHILLING

These are places where you can sit and enjoy a conversation with your friends, over drinks and bar foods. Similarly, some of these are great for couples looking to get away from meat-markets and wanting a more romantic evening.

BAR HOPING AREAS

The most popular bar hopping areas in Salvador are Rio Vermelho, Pelourinho and Ribeira (though this last one operates during the day mostly).

If, however, you want to paint the town red and visit several spots in one night, we recommend you hire a guide instead of cabbing back and forth.
Justin Edu (Georgia)
justlloyd@hotmail.com
8128-0461
call or email for prices and tour options

APPROACH INDEX:

The potential for approaching someone (or being approached by someone) is rated here on our personal experiences. 1= mostly couples sitting down, 5= mostly singles out on the hunt, standing and dancing.

CONSUMPTION CARD SYSTEM

The control card most clubs hand you as you walk in is called a consuption card. On it, the bartender marks what you order. Before leaving the place, you go to the cashier and pay for everything you had. This way, you don't have to handle money during your night, nor do you tip in excess. They will add 10% as an automatic tip to the waiter. Note: Do not lose the card as they will fine you over R$100 to allow you to leave their establishment.

AFTER-HOURS

Most trailler-beer-vendors will serve you till you can't take it no-mo'. If you want to drink amongst people, Mercado do Peixe in Rio Vermelho is a sure shot any day of the week.

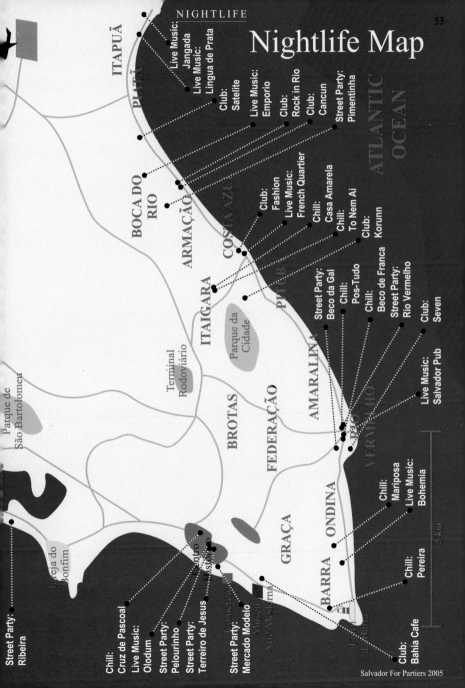

Nightlife Map

ITAPUÃ

PLATÃ

ATLANTIC OCEAN

Live Music: Jangada

Live Music: Lingua de Prata

Club: Satelite

Live Music: Emporio

Club: Rock in Rio

Club: Cancun

Street Party: Pimentinha

BOCA DO RIO

ARMAÇÃO

COSTA AZUL

Club: Fashion

Live Music: French Quartier

Chill: Casa Amarela

Chill: To Nem Ai

Club: Korunn

ITAIGARA

PITUBA

Parque da Cidade

Street Party: Beco da Gal

Chill: Pos-Tudo

Chill: Beco de Franca

Street Party: Rio Vermelho

Club: Seven

Terminal Rodoviário

BROTAS

FEDERAÇÃO

AMARALINA

RIO VERMELHO

Live Music: Salvador Pub

Parque de São Bartolomeu

Chill: Mariposa

Live Music: Bohemia

Igreja do Bonfim

GRAÇA

ONDINA

BARRA

Chill: Pereira

Street Party: Ribeira

Chill: Cruz de Pascoal

Live Music: Olodum

Street Party: Pelourinho

Street Party: Terreiro de Jesus

Street Party: Mercado Modelo

Museu Arte Moderna

Club: Bahia Cafe

Sunday Night- Clubbing

FASHION CLUB

One of Salvador's true clubs, with two floors, a DJ stage, large dance floor and sofas around the side seat the rich, college crowd. Get here early as the entrance overpacks after 11pm.

Dress up. (ages 18 to 35) approach index: 4 Get there at: 10pm
Av. Otavio Mangabeira 2471, Jd. Namorados

Sunday Night- Street Party

TERREIRO DE JESUS

There is always a few bands performing for free in Pelourinho every Sunday. Every now and then, a major name shows up. Ask around on Saturday as most of the city will know if it's someone famous.

Dress casual. (ages 18 to 55) approach index: 4 Get there at: 7pm
Terreiro de Jesus, Pelourinho

Sunday Night- Live Music

BOHEMIA PILSEN BAR

Nice traditional bar with live music (Axe) early every Sunday, starting at 1pm going on till late. A perfect post-beach hang out with great food (seafood)

Dress down. (ages 21 to 35) approach index: 4 Get there at: 5pm
Rua Belo Horizonte 177, Jardim Brasil

Sunday Night- Chilling

MARIPOSA

A cozy and well decorated street corner house with over 30 crepes on the menu. Great to meet new people or to hang with friends. Dress up yet comfortably. (ages 25 to 35) approach index: 3 Get there at: 8pm. Dress up/casual. (ages 21 to 35) approach index: 3 Get there at: 9pm
Rua Professor Sabino Silva 14, Jardim Apipema

Monday Night- Clubbing

ROCK IN RIO

Large, late 90's industrial style club safely located inside the Aero-Club mall. The club switches between DJ and live music on a daily basis. No one goes home alone. Dress up. (ages 18 to 35) approach index: 4 Get there at: 10pm
Shopping AeroClube

Monday Night- Street Party

BAR RIBEIRA - SEGUNDA GORDA

You have to see it to believe: everyone (bosses included) cutting work to go party on a regular Monday afternoon. All the beach kiosks are packed with those who know that life`s too short for work.

Dress beach style. (ages 18 to 45) approach index: 5 Get there at: 1pm(!)
Praia de Ribeira

Monday Night- Live Music

JANGADA

Beach kiosk style bar with live Pagode. Dress casual. (ages 18 to 45) approach index: 5 Get there at: 8pm
Praia de Itapoan

Monday Night- Chilling

PEREIRA

Designer architecture, chilled indoor area, tabled balcony and one of Salvador's finset cuisines sets this lounge apart. Dress up. (ages 25 to 45) approach index: 2 Get there at: 9pm
Av. Sete de Setembro 3959, Porto da Barra

Tuesday Night- Clubbing

CAFE CANCUN

Mexican themed decorations, although the band or DJ will vary according to the night. Tuesday is salsa night, and only a few know how to dance it. The rest make up their moves borrowed from forro. Dress up. (ages 18 to 35) approach index: 4 Get there at: 10pm
AeroClub Shopping

Tuesday Night- Street Party

LIVE SHOW AT TERREIRO DE JESUS

Every Tuesday there is a live show with a different guest artist.

Dress casual. (ages 18 to 55) approach index: 4 Get there at: 7pm
Terreiro de Jesus, Pelourinho

Tuesday Night- Live Music

OLODUM AT PELOURINHO

Oludum has been playing at Pelourinho for the last decade and amazing both tourists and locals with their empowering drum troupe. A definite must. Dress casual. (ages 18 to 55) approach index: 5 Get there at: 10pm
Pelourinho

Tuesday Night- Chilling

CRUZ DO PASCOAL

This secret little dive's balcony has several tables facing a great view of the bay from the higher city. Stupidly cold beers and bar foods, such as the "aipim com carne seca". Dress casual (ages 18 to 55) approach index: 1 Get there at: 10pm
Rua Joaquim Tavora 2, Cruz do Pascoal, St. Antonio

Wednesday Night- Clubbing

TROPICANA

A large show-house with a dance floor for whenever the band is late. Lots of young people wanting forro, samba and pagode. Dress casual. (ages 20 to 35) approach index: 5 Get there at: 10pm
Av. Otavio Mangabeira 4707, Jd. Armação

Wednesday Night- Street Party

BECO DA GAL

Though not necessarily a free street party (there is a nominal fee of R$5pp), it feels like one, specially since it takes place in an alley. Great pagode and samba all night. Dress down (ages 25 to 40) approach index: 3 Get there at: 10pm
Do Lado do Perinni do Rio Vermelho

Wednesday Night- Live Music

FRENCH QUARTIER

A ritzy jazz club that will help put all Brazilian music in perspective. Wednesdays is Bossanova night, Brazil`s contribution to jazz. Behaved clientele, superior menu. Dress up. (ages 28 to 55) approach index: 1 Get there at: 9pm
Av. Otavio Mangabeira 2323, Jd. Namorados

Wednesday Night- Chilling

TO NEM AI

Considered one of the best happy-hours in Salvador, with every right: outdoor tables, airy and cozy environment where everyone yaps at the same time. Great food. Dress casual. (ages 18 to 35) approach index: 2 Get there at: 7pm
Rua das Hortencias 248, Pituba

Thursday Night- Clubbing

KORUNN

One of those neon and black-light clubs with a few bars, dancefloors and a stage for where the DJ takes care of all. Dress up. (ages 20 to 35) approach index: 4 Get there at: 10pm
Rua Ceara 1240, Pituba

Thursday Night- Street Party

RIO VERMELHO

There is always people in Rio Vermelho`s triangle, specially since Dinha is there attracting everyone with one Bahia`s best acarajes. Out door tables from various bars. Starts off as a happy hour and goes on till 1am.

Dress casual. (ages 18 to 45) approach index: 3 Get there at: 8pm
Acaraje da Dinha, Rio Vermelho

Thursday Night- Live Music

SALVADOR PUB

Why is an English pub in Salvador being recommended Wel, first, you may be home sick, second, you may want tobe sick of arrocha music, third, its got great food and lounge/jazz music performed live on Thursdays. Dress up. (ages 30 to 50) approach index: 2 Get there at: 9pm

Rua do Meio 154, Rio Vermelho

Thursday Night- Chilling

POS-TUDO

An upstairs sit-down bar right next to Rio Vermelho`s street action, ideal if you want proper bar food and a little live music in the back. Dress casual. (ages 22 to 40) approach index: 2 Get there at: 10pm

Rua Joao Gomes 87, Rio Vermelho

Friday Night- Clubbing

SATELITE

An Ibiza type club, next to the beach (although no access) with international djs playing eletronic music. The internation crowd will make you feel more at home, if that`s what you want. Dress up. (ages 20 to 35) approach index: 4 Get there at: 10pm

Av. Otavio Mangabeira 940, Patamares

Friday Night- Street Party

PAGODE AT MERCADO MODELO

Though more of a happy hour than a night spot, this pagode session is great to understand how Brazilians like to sing and dance along to their favourite songs. Dress casual. (ages 18 to 40) Approach index: 3 Get there at: 6pm

Mercado Modelo, Comercio

Friday Night- Live Music

Lingua de Prata

...agode and Aroxa is performed every Friday at Lingua de Prata, a ca-
...ana style bar on the coast. Dress casual. (ages 18 to 35) approach in-
...ex: 3 Get there at: 10pm
...raia de Itapuan

Friday Night- Chilling

Casa Amarela

A quaint and well decorated sit-
down bar house, with out-door tables. Right next door to To Nem Ai
(Wed-chill).

Dress up. (ages 18 to 35) approach
index: 4 Get there at: 10pm
Rua das Hortencias 260, Pituba

Saturday Night- Clubbing

BAHIA CAFE

A beautiful up-scale club/bar with a balcony packed with tables offering a full view of the bay. One of Brazil`s best clubs given the music, view, decor and service. Live music followed by a DJ. Dress your best. (ages 25 to 40) approach index: 3 Get there at: 10pm
Largo dos Aflitos, Aflitos

Saturday Night- Street Party

PIMENTINHA

A shanty-town architecture to this bizarrely decorated two story bar. As you enter, a wizard will bless your sole with leaves and popcorn. Opt for the fresher upper deck, even if the floor shakes with each step. If too packed, just hang around outside in the street party. Dress casual. (ages 24 to 45) approach index: 3 Get there at: 9pm
Rua Dom Eugenio Sales 11, Boca do Rio

aturday Night- Live Music

MPORIO

it-down bars butted up right next to each other, so you can hop to
next that gets going. Most will have some type of live music, but
ones on the ends have live music and a dance floor.

ss casual. (ages 25 to 55) approach index: 4 Get there at: 9pm
Jorge Amado 300, Imbui

aturday Night- Chilling

BOTECO DO FRANÇA

This alley bar located in Rio Vermelho is adjacent to various other night spots, should you want to change
your pace.Dress casual. (ages 22 to 35) approach index: 3 Get there at: 8pm
Rua Borges dos Reis 24, Rio Vermelho

GAY SALVADOR

by Claudio Sampaio

Just like any major metropolitan area, Salvador has a very active gay life: most homosexuals from smaller cities move here because they find refuge in the big city.

However, there are differences. For starters, gays are a lot more socially mixed amongst straight people: there is mutual respect from their families, neighbors and co-workers. This all means that you can be as gay as you want and you won't get egged on (as long as you don't irritate others). Similarly, there is no need for a gay pride parade, as it is celebrated extensively before and during carnival.

This is also one of the reasons why there isn't a gay residential neighborhood. Barra, however, does have a gay block, with bars and clubs dominating the area.

HOW TO DRESS

Dress whatever you always wanted: whether it is neutral or drag, you can do so here at any of the clubs without annoying anyone: Locals are used to transvestites, butch lesbians, clown drags etc.

LOVE

One word of advice: there are a bunch of gay prostitutes around the city. Should you fall in love and want to bring him/her back, watch out for your stuff in the hotel room. You are better off taking the person to a motel, where you won't stand a chance of losing anything nor irritating the concierge.

As far as continuing your relationship, just remember this: Brazilians love Brazil. Most don't want to move anywhere else. This means that in case you fall in love and should that someone fall in love back, you could start planning to move this way instead of the other way round (unless you have loads of money).

Salvador for Partiers 2005

EX

lthough people here kiss faster
an most places in the world,
ey are not as promiscuous as
ne would imagine. You may se-
al kiss during the night and still
o home alone.

he bath houses are a mix of a
lub and brothel, where anything
oes if you spend you money
ght.

STREETS & PARKS

venida Sete de Setembro
rom Campo Grande to Praça da Sé ,
lostly next to Praça da Piedade , lots
f flirting

ua Carlos Gomes
rom Largo 2 de Julho to Campo Grande

raça Pedro Arcanjo and 2M
elourinho

BATH HOUSES

Sauna Rio's
Almeida Sande , 8
Barris
71) 328-3275

Sauna Olympus
Rua Tuiuti , 183
Centro) Carlos Gomes
71) 329-0060

Sauna Persona
Rua Junqueira Aires , 230
Barris
(71) 329-1273

Sauna Phoenix
Rua Prados Valadares , 16
Nazaré
(71) 326-4585 / (71) 243-5495

Sauna Campos
Rua Dias D'Ávila , 25
Farol da Barra
(71) 235-2247

Esgrima
Ladeira de Santa Tereza , 2
Centro
(71) 322-3813 / (71) 321-2708

Termas Omni
Rua Augusto França , 22
Dois de Julho
(71) 321-9044

NIGHT SPOTS

OFF Club
Rua Dias D' Ávila , 33
Farol da Barra
(71) 267-6215

YES
Rua Gamboa de Cima , 24
Gamboa

Caverna
Rua Carlos Gomes , 616
Centro
(71) 358-2410

Festa
Farol da Barra , s/n.
Barra

Clube Gay QUEENS
Rua Teodoro Sampio , 160
Barris
(71) 328-6220 / (71) 328-5766
www.queensclube.com.br

BARS & RESTAURANTS

CAMARIN e BANANA BRASIL
Rua Leovigildo Filgueira , Beco dos
Artistas s/n
Garcia.

CHARLES CHAPLIN BAR
Rua Carlos Gomes , 140
Centro
(71) 247-5881

TOUCHE CREPERIA
Rua Belo Horizonte
Jardim Brasil-Barra
(71) 9121-9084

ÂNCORA DO MARUJO
Rua Senador Costa Pinto , 80
Carlos Gomes

SEX SHOPS

The Dreams
(71) 247-4122

Queens
(71) 328-6220

Ritual Sex Shop
(71) 240-1073

BEACH SPOTS

Farol da Barra (On saturdays)

Praia dos Artistas
Boca do Rio (On sundays).
Tend : Aruba

EVENTS
Gay Pride Parade
June

DATING

How to deal with

By India Lee Borba

It is now time for you to see what Brazil has to offer you when it comes to the men department. We have all heard of `Latin Lovers,` but what does that mean exactly? Here are the answers to questions you ever had about Brazilian men and where to meet them.

Brazilian women usually meet men through mutual friends. So, get out there and make some Brazilian friends. You never know who they could introduce you to. Brazilians are open, friendly and helpful people, and when it comes to conversation, Locals have no shame. So, exchange phone numbers or emails and make plans to meet again.

In Brazil, the men are very fond of public affection and are expert romantics. So, grab a caipirinha and ask someone to teach you to dance the Samba or Forró. Get ready to be close, because the Brazilians will have it no other way when it comes to dancing.

The men will tell you how beautiful you are, or for that matter, that you are the most beautiful woman they have ever seen!

Don't be surprised if you are lip-locked within the first 5 minutes of your conversation and be prepared about the motels. Remember that in Brazil, motels are for one thing, and one thing only. Sex! You have the power to accept the proposal or not, but just know what you are agreeing to.

No matter which type you choose, the important thing is to have fun and don't go falling in love on the first night!

When you are trying to relax on the beach, you are sure to be approached by at least one of the types, most likely, the Hippie. These docile men, will try to sell you a necklace or maybe even make you a free ring that costs less than 50 cents. But, it's the thought that counts right?

If you are in a bar or club, a man may even send over his friend to tell you he thinks you are cute or send a note! This may sound juvenile to you, but it is considered normal here in Brazil.

Don't feel obligated to speak to every man who comes your way. If the men think that you are easy, you will be batting them away the whole evening which can get quite annoying.

Dos and Don'ts

Here are a few dos and don'ts that should help you along.

Don't hesitate to accept the offer of a kiss from any man who strikes your fancy.

Do come armed with a pen and paper to ensure you will be able to pass out your phone number and email address, but don't expect them to call the next day.

Do keep a positive attitude and play it cool when the annoying guy at the end of the bar won't take a hint and give up.

Do ask a cute Salvadorian to show you around their beautiful city.

Don't believe them when they tell you that you are the women of their dreams no matter how much you want to.

Don't be surprised if you go to the motel and your man pays for it by the hour.

Do contact the author if you are looking for a nice, caring, gentle latin lover. Major credit cards accepted. Joke.

BRAZILIAN BOYS

Brazil is full of these beautiful, tan, athletic ´eye candy` and they come in 4 different flavors.

Reminder: These are gross generalizations and should not be taken too seriously.

THE TOURIST

It happens on every vacation: you meet someone from your own neighbourhood. Should you waste your precious time on someone from your own back yard? Well, if they have the same tour goals as you, why not? You can take a schooner tour the next day, share cabs and maybe a room in Morro de Sao Paulo! Rrrrrr!

THE BEER POSER

He's tanned, he's got big lips, a beer is always in his hand and he's looking at you. Now he may not be the sexiest thing in the world, and you may not be impressed by the arrocha music blasting out his car speaker, but he can sure make out, dance and the rest.

THE DANCER

He can dance to any type of music, thanks to his african roots. And if they can dance well, they can do other moves just as well. Should you dance with him? Of course! You are in Bahia, and you can be an observer or you can experience.

THE PLAYBOY

Last, but no least, we have the Playboy who can also be found at the trendy nightlife scene. They prefers talking about money and women, and how to get more of either! These are the eligible bachelors and ultimate players. They know what we want, and they have the ability to give it to us.

HOW TO DEAL WITH

Everybody in Salvador loves sex. It's in the air. More so than the rest of Brazil. This does not mean they are easy. it means that when its on, its on.

Salvador boys are always reminding them of how hot they look. These boys are very aggressive in their approach to seduction, meaning that these women have had to naturally build a hard shell around them, otherwise they would be picked up left and right and end up being treated like a whore.

The best places to meet them are during any of the live music shows that get people dancing (arrocha, forro, pagode, samba, axe etc), as opposed to bossa-nova and MPB. To meet tourists, your best bet is to either stay in a young hotel, inn or hostel, to take group tours or to wander in Pelourinho for a few hours.

Most Salvadorian women still live with their parents, since Salvador is a dangerous city for a girl to live alone. This means that you won't be invited back to their place. You will, however, get to kiss them within 30 minutes of talking with them, sometimes a lot faster than that. If things go really well and the chemistry works out, you can take them to a motel for a two hours session. But just a reminder: kissing them does not guarantee that you will be sleeping with them, as it is common in Europe and the US. You may be making out with a serial kisser.

Should you catch yourself in a more meaningful conversation with a Brazilian girl, your next move is naturally to shag. Since there are few love nooks in Salvador, like cute little alleys, safe parks or beaches, your best bet is to bring her back to your hotel (if the concierge hasn't mentioned any policies against that) or to take her to a motel. Since you are probably moving around in a cab, the procedure is to tell the cab driver which motel you want to go while she is stepping in the car. That way she won't feel embarassed. If you are in Morro de Sao Paulo or Praia do Forte, you can just find a secluded beach.

Meanwhile, should she not want to sleep with you, you may ask for her digits or email. Unfortunately, it is probably unlikely that anything will develop, since most of these girls have no problem finding a boy for their night the next time they go out.

RULES

What does all this mean for you? This means your approach should take some of these factors into consideration:

1) Don't hit on them at the beach, unless the beach is relatively empty. (Forget it on weekends.)

2) Don't bother trying to pick them up in the street.

3) Do persist a little. Most women in Brazil are so used to being hit on every 15 minutes that they don't appreciate any half-assed attempt anymore.

4) A good conversation starter is to ask them about their opinion on touristy spots. Show this book and ask them what they recommend.

5) Do try to make out as soon as you can.

6) Don't insist on going back to their place. Do suggest a drive along Jardim dos Namorados (where most of the better motels are).

BRAZILIAN WOMEN

The Main Types

The 4 types of Brazilian woman (other than the normal chick):

THE BRITNEY SPEARS:

They are daddy's little girl, they dress like Britney Spears, they look great but they don't let anyone hit on them. Why? They have a huge waiting list of suitors from their former high-school, their college, their parent's friend's sons etc etc. They CAN be stuck up. Forget them, unless you are introduced to one.

THE POPOZUDA:

Big-butted sex machines. They work out, wear tight pants that ride up their butt, dye their hair blond and do their best to look like a bomb-shell. Good to invest your time on, since the motel is always a possibility with these honeys.

THE "TOO-EASY" GIRL

She may not ask for money up-front, but she will put all her drinks on your bill. She may order for her friends too. You won't know if she likes you or your wallet until too late. To test, ask if there is a motel around here, and if she wants to go. If so, she may also state her price, and you'll know what you are dealing with.

Legal disclaimer: Prostitution is illegal in Brazil.

THE TOURIST

They may not have the best asses or the nicest clothes, in their effort to be less tempting to street elements, but they need someone too. Your surest way to get them to tag along is to see if they are aware of all the street parties going on in Salvador. If not, make them seem like they have been missing out, and invite them to one, right now!

FOR THE GIRLS
Beauty and personal hygiene
By Laira Hordones Lemos

Beauty salons are relatively cheap in Brazil, compared to 1st world countries.

So, once in Brazil, plan a pit-stop in one of them. Manicure costs around US$3, so you should do your nails and toes using light colors during summer and maybe red during our so-called winter. But above all, you should do some waxing, if you haven't shaved just before. Brazilians wax all around their bodies, so probably there'll be plenty of hair left on you.

"BRAZILIAN" WAXING

Start with your upper lips "buço" (mandatory if there's any hair, even the invisible ones) and your eyebrows "sobrancelhas" (can be done with a tweezers or waxing). Then do your underarms and your legs. Now bikini waxing may hurt a little bit, but you feel a lot "cleaner" afterwards, and besides it will last 3 to 4 weeks, a lot longer than shaving, not to mention they will reach into those hard-to-shave spots.

There are 3 options for bikini waxing:

1) **virilha**: the ordinary groin waxing, just on the bits that your bikini can't hide. You won't need to take your bikini or panties off. Just hold it to where you want it waxed. Wear a skirt or dress to make it easier.

2) **virilha contorno**: the sides and the back so you can lean down to pick up something.

3) **Virilha cavada**: highly recommended. They'll wax everything except the front part. The lady who is supposed to explain and ask you up to where she can go, will be using gloves and disposable wax, so it's completely safe. You'll be thanking this lady for the following month every time you shower or have sex.

HAIRCUT

Now-a-days you will probably see more blondes than brunettes in Brazil. They'll be 10% natural and 90% fake, though some will look perfectly natural. Besides this blonde fashion, there's also the brushing: 60% of the girls will go out at night with very straight hairs. If you have curly hair this is your chance to give it a try since it is cheap here (US$5 to 10), depending on the salon.

There will be beauty salons in every corner of the main streets in Salvador. If you are staying in the main neighborhoods, take a walk on their respective main streets (Leblon: Av. Ataulfo de Paiva; Ipanema: Av. Visconde Pirajá; Copacabana: Av. N. Sra. Copacabana) and choose the salon that you like the best. To make your choice easier, there's a list with price ranges, phones and addresses below. The most

famous are Werner and Giorgio. At Werner, like most of them, you'll have to call in advance (1 day) and book a time for what you want. At Giorgio, in Ipanema, you don´t have to book a time, just show up (you may have to wait a little bit, 5 to 10 min).

No waiting sallon lane
A great place to go to get your hair done where you won't have to wait in line is a strip mall with a dozen hair sallons on Rua Alm. Marques Leao in Barra. (Marques Leao with Brito Lemos).

Jacques Janine
Shopping da Barra

Pura Beleza
Barra

HIGHLIGHTS

Salvador is also a good place to take the opportunity to highlight your hair. One of the best is Werner, priced around R$200 (US$70), They are expensive, but known as the best. That's why you'll need to book a time with him. Don't be late, and save 2 hours for the job. He can make you look like a goddess, or anything else you want.

FACIALS

Many salons may also offer facials, which are not really recommended till your last few days here, since you may get marks that last for a whole week.

What to wear

Brazil is a country with a peculiar way of dressing, and Salvador is where you can see this most clearly. That is because although fashion is universal, only certain types of clothing adapt in the country, and those are mainly the ones that have sex appeal and aren't too warm.

Always look for the tighter pants and the shorter shirts. Loose clothes are currently not a big hit in Salvador. Colors can be freely chosen, although the bright ones are kept for summer. High heeled boots and sandals are very welcome, although low sandals are used all year round.

During the summer is when Salvador girls show off what they have worked on their bodies all year long. You'll see lots of flat tummies, short skirts, low cuts, etc. Since locals stay at the beach until 7pm, you'll see lots of beach wear on the streets at night.

Your bikini and kanga will be your outfit for lunch and walking on the street, and even to go to the mall, with a top and maybe a skirt when necessary. That will work for any event you have during the day in Salvador: day parties, barbecues, lunches, ecotourism, shopping, and of course, the beach.

The main outfit for the beach right now is bikini under a tight top and skirt. But anything will work: short dresses, shorts, kangas, etc, even a light long dress.

During a summer night girls may look nothing different from how they look during the day. There will be no heavy make up or big hair, and hardly any fancy outfit, unless there is a fancy party or wedding. There may be some big earrings or necklaces, but not both. For the shoes, there will be plenty of high heel sandals as well as just slippers. Aside from the accessories, outfits can be detailed into 3 main occasions:

1) CLUBS:

For clubs, you may see tops and shirts/pants in some sort of shining fabric, sleeveless dresses and tops, lots of low-cut black outfits, necklaces, shining color tops, and plenty of high heels. Usually the strongest sex appeal clothing are worn at night clubs.

Recommended Shops:
Zoomp
Forum
Yes Brasil

(all found in Shopping Iguatemi and Shopping da Barra)

2) STREET PARTIES:

On open-air parties there are really no rules except to dress casual and sexy. You'll see all sorts of this mix, and they will be adapted to any "tribe" taste: the hippies, the preppies, the surfers, the classic ones. This will usually mean: any top, with any pants/skirt, and any sandal. Many girls will even wear their bikini tops.

Recommended Shops:
Cantao
Sartore
TNG

(all found in Shopping Iguatemi)

3) BARS AND LIVE MUSIC:

This is an "in between" outfit of the clubs and the streets. If it's an indoor bar, then it's similar to clubs, with a little less shine If it's an outdoor bar, or a live music event, then it's just like the street-parties fashion. Be sure to check out a clothes store called Vero, run by a friend of mine, and one of the best deals in town for the 20 something crowd.

Recommended Shops:
Lells Blanc
Tritton
M. Officer

Just remember that anything you wear has to be extremely light, because no matter what, it will be very hot everywhere.

SAFETY TIPS:

For a Brazilian metroplitan area, Salvador is very safe. Most of the touristic areas are well guarded, and the people in general are extremely friendly towards tourists. In nearby destinations such as Praia do Forte or Morro de Sao Paulo, you would proably have to beg someone to steal from you. Most of these villages live off tourism and everyone understands that for every $10 stolen, they lose $400 in lost clients.

Given that Salvador's nightlife are spread out, you'll be cabbing safely back and forth at night. However, care should be taken in the neighbourhoods around Pelourinho and the historic center, as those are less policed.

Beware on empty streets just as much as at overly crowded events. The new age in pick pocketing (some new Eastern-European techniques are now arriving in Brazil) is to create a situation in a crowd where your hands are distracted while they go for your pockets.

A common trick here in Brazil is the "fight breaks out" trick, when right in front of you there is a scuffle in the middle of a crowd. While everyone is being pushed away from the scuffle, and while you are holding someone who is being pushed onto you, someone behind you (sometimes a woman) goes through your pockets.

Don't be a hero: if you are held at gun point, slowly pass over the money, turn around and walk fast (don't run) and leave it at that.

Get the hell out after any dangerous situation: if you managed to stop a pick pocket in his tracks, get out, as his partners may come after you.

If you are passing by a shady character in an empty street at night, wave an eager "Hi! I'm over here!" to your imaginary friend that's a block away. This should throw a monkey wrench in his scheme at the last second.

If you get pick-pocketed, say what-the-hell and go on with your tour instead of getting caught up in reporting incidents and other red tape. Not only is that an exercise of futility, but it will eat up your time and mood. Like a friend of mine said after getting $200 pick-pocketed in the north of Brazil: "Fuck it, I consider it a small tourist tax" and went back to drinking. Not the best point of view as a long-term philosophy, but it worked fine that week.

Local

How to avoid being a target

As a general rule, you want to dress down. The grungy look will do you good. Since you are on vacation, you don't need to worry about your reputation or poor service. Here are some general rules to abide by, to better guarantee your safety (specially when anywhere between Flamengo and Centro or the north side):

BASEBALL CAPS

Dead give-aways.

HAIR CUT

Leave the "out of control" waxed hair style for the trendier clubs.

ACCENT

When in a crowd of dubious types, keep your talking to a minimum.

BACK-PACK

Another dead give-away. Do you really need it? You don't need to carry a 2 liter water bottle, specially when they sell a chilled one in every corner.

SHIRT

T-shirt instead of a hawaiian shirt. Leave the Brazilian soccer team shirt for back home.

MONEY & IDS

Don't bring too much nor too little money, as they will shake you down till they get something. Don't carry a passport, nor all your credit cards or more than R$200. bring one major cc and one form of ID: student, drivers' license or state. Don't trust your pockets, keep them zipped or buttoned up.

CAMERA

Don't walk around thinking the strap will guarantee your camera's safety.

BERMUDAS

You can wear bermudas, but wear the styles the Brazilian boys wear (beach bermuda), not what's in style back home (the one with a built-in belt).

SANDALS

Wear shoes or flip-flops instead.

Gringo

STREET FOODS

ACARAJE

The omni-present king of all street snacks in Bahia: Black-eye pea cake deep fried in palm oil, then filled with dried shrimp, vatapa and okra , all optional. Reject the peppers or you`ll die ("sem pimenta!").

ABARA

A banana-leaf-steamed Acaraje. Good for those avoiding deep-fried stuff.

BOLINHO DE ESTUDANTE

A dry tapioca pressed into shape, grilled then rolled in cinamon sugar.

PÃO DE QUEIJO:

Cheese puffs like you never had them before. Absolute must.

PASTEL DE CARNE:

Very much like a deep fried ground beef wonton. Must try.

EMPADA DE CAMARÃO:

Shrimp cup pastry.

KIBE:

Arabic snack made from deep fried whole-wheat surrounding a spicy ground beef center.

AND SNACKS

COXINHA:
String chicken pastry inside deep-fried dough.

BOLINHO DE AIPIM:
Deep-fried cassava dough with a ground beef center.

CACHORRO QUENTE (HOT DOG):
A variation of the NY style hotdog: bread, hot dog link, tomato paste with onions and peppers, then optionals: corn, string potatoes, parmesan and other stuff. Forget the other stuff.

ESFIHA:
A tri-folded pizza of Arabic origin. Must have.

CHURROS:
Deep fried dough filled with none other than doce de leite (caramel's rich cousin). Then rolled in cinnamon sugar. Mmmmm good.

MISTO QUENTE:
Ham and cheese sandwich, made with stringy mozzarella. A must and usually very safe.

X-TUDO:
Double cheese burger with everything they have to offer: bacon, fried egg, sausage, pulled chicken, string potatoes, etc etc.

PASTEL DE FORNO:
Oven baked folded pie with various flavor fillings. Great usually.

BOLINHO DE BACALHAU:
Cod fish cake in ball format. Very good. Eat it with olive oil. Don't try the peppers.

BAR FOODS

PORÇÃO DE PASTEIS

Portion of the deep fried wontons, comes in different flavors (beef, cheese, shrimp or Cornish cheese)

PORÇÃO DE BOLINHO DE BACALHAU

Portion of cod fish cakes.

AIPIM FRITO

Deep fried cassava, a stringy cousin of the potato.

CARNE SECA COM AIPIM FRITO

Just like Aipim Frito but with sun dried jerked meat, very popular.

CALDO DE FEIJÃO

Bean soup with bacon bits.

PEIXE ASSADO

Simple, baked fish. Non-filling, so a bar food.

ACARAJE

Available in as a sandwish or as a dish, in most out-door bars, beach kiosks and street parties.

LAMBRETA

Mussels in various flavours: spicy, lemon, cheese etc. They come in dozens and the world record is 1440 in one afternoon.

CAMARAO A MILANESA

Breaded shrimp. Ask for "camarao pistola", the larger shrimp.

BOLINHO DE PEIXE

Fish cakes.

DESSERTS

f you are into desserts and all things sweet, you can't miss any of these, all of them Brazilian, all very, very sweet. (Sugar was so common in colonial Brazil that it had be used in abundance).

COCADA

Coconut slivers connect by sugar and love. Available in regular or burnt coconut flavours.

BEIJU

A tapioca pancake filled with condensed milk, doce de leite or honey. Awesome.

BRIGADEIRO

Condensed milk meets chocolate on the stove, then is rolled into a ball and sprinkled with…chocolate sprinkles… must try.

PUDIM DE LEITE

Just like a "flan", but sweeter.

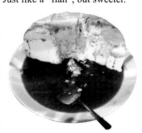

PUDIM DE CLARA

Before egg whites and sugar become a meringue, it becomes a pudim de clara, a very soft, sweet and airy pudim. A must for sweet-toothed people.

DOCE DE LEITE DE CABRA

Clumpy goat milk doce de leite (caramel's rich cousin), eaten with cheese.

FRUIT SALAD

If you are not into sweet stuff, then a tropical fruit salad is in order.

CUSCUS

Tapioca pudding in a stiffer form, topped with happiness` very own condensed milk.

DOCE DE GOIABA

It's not an ear, but sweet guava preserve in syrup. Eat it with cheese.

STUFF YOU

All these things can be found in your local super-market (Bom Preco,

DOCE DE LEITE

Caramel's cousin, but sweater, darker and creamier. Made from sugar and milk. Try it in bar and paste form

GELEIA DE MOCOTÓ

Sweet bone-marrow jello, but definitely fun to eat. (Squeeze it between your teeth and cheek.)

(Reg. Trademark Arisco SA)

DANONINHO

A thickened-up yogurt so small you must eat with the tiniest spoon available (borrow Barbie's).

(Reg. Trademark Danone LTDA)

YAKULT

Fermented milk with a zing to it. For kids, but adults also love it.

(Reg. Trademark -Yacult LTDA)

TORRONE

A chewy bar with peanuts or cashew nuts. Italian origin, but now nationalized in Brazil.

BOMBOM GAROTO

A box with an assortment of different bon-bons and miniature chocolate bars. Great to have at the hotel.

(Reg. Trademark- Chocolate Garoto S.A)

NEVER ATE

Perini). They all make great gifts for your friends and family.

PALMITO- HEART OF PALM

The center of a Palm tree's trunk. Buy a jar and eat them straight. If you don't like it, send it to me.

COCADA

Coconut slivers mixed with sugary ligament. Very, very sweet.

AMENDOIM JAPONÊS

Japanese peanuts. Peanuts covered with a crunchy shell. Great to have around at all times.

(Reg. Trademark AGTAL A. Guedes Torrefação de Amendoim LTDA)

BOLACHAS

Cookies.

(Reg. Trademark Bauduco & Cia LTDA)

BISCOITO DE POLVILHO

The best alternative to potato chips. Oven baked, containing very little fat. Great at the beach (ask for biscoito Globo, or wave to the guy with a big plastic bag).

(Reg. Trademark Pan. Mandarino LTDA)

PAÇOQUINHA

Peanut powder compressed into a bar. Very good.

PÉ DE MOLEQUE

Peanut brittle. Roasted peanuts joined by hardened molasses.

EVERYTHING YOU

Alcoholic
(Let's talk about these first)

CERVEJA

From an international point of view, all Brazilian beers taste the same: they are all lagers or pilsners, as any other type of beer would not agree with the weather. When given an option, ask for Skol.

CAIPIRINHA

The most refreshing alcoholic mixed-drink in the world! Cachaca, lime, sugar and ice. Great at any occasion: bar, restaurant, clubbing, breakfast. Just don't buy it from street vendors, as they sometime use ice made from water that can make you sick. Also, try the caipiroska (aka caipivodka), made with vodka and the caipisake (with sake, duh). And some trendier places offer it with different fruits: pineapple, strawberry, tangerine, seriguela etc. When given a choice of cachaca, opt for the ones from the north of Minas Gerais or from Salinas.

CRAVINHO

Cachaça (pr: casha-ssa= Brazilian rum) aged in oak barrels with cloves and other flavours.

CAPETA

Guarana powder (stimulant) rum, condensed milk and any choice of fruit all blended to make a very sweet and tasty cocktail that`s very hard to get drunk to. Ideal for girls.

CHOPP

A light beer on tap. Normally preferred over bottled beer.

BATIDA DE CÔCO

Very smooth drink, will get you drunk without you knowing it. Coconut milk, rum, sugar and other stuff all blended into a milkshake.

CHILEAN WINES

While down here, go for the affordable Santa Carolina, or the full bodied Casileiro Del Diablo from Concha&Toro. Given the heat, an espumante may also make more sense, if a bucket of ice is available.

HOULD DRINK

Non Alcoholic

GUARANÁ

The most popular Brazilian soft drink, great at any occasion.

(Reg. Trademark AmBev SA LTDA)

AGUA DE COCO:

Coconut water, not milk. Very good for whenever you are de-hydrating. 2 will cure most hang-overs.

REDBULL

RedBull, Flying Horse, Burn etc. are all energy drinks. Ideal after the late-afternoon siesta.(Pronounced Hedge-Boo)

(Reg. Trademark RedBull GmbH)

MATE

A deep iced tea from the south of Brazil, made from the mate herb. Available in diet and regular/ natural or lemon flavoured.

(Reg. Trademark Leão LTDA)

AGUA

Since tap water is not potable in Brazil, you should always look for water bottles. SEM gas= non-carbonated, COM gas= car-bonated.

(Reg. Trademark Alimentos e Bebidas Campos do Jordão LTDA)

ADES JUICES

Tasty soy milk juices made from various fruits, normally found in super-markets.

(Reg. Trademark Unilever Best Foods Brasil LTDA)

FRUITS AND JUICES

MANGA —MANGO

Considered by many the one fruit they would take with them to a desert island, had they only one choice.
Sweet and creamy. Vitamin A and C.

GOIABA- GUAVA

Thick, sweet and smooth, just like me. Vitamin A, C and complex B and other minerals. Not recommended for those with digestive problems.

MAMÃO - PAPAYA

Just as healthy as the avocado, papaya milk shake is great for your intestinal works. Vitamin A and C, a natural laxative and stress reliever.

MARACUJÁ- PASSION FRUIT

Slightly bitter to a point that it makes your cheeks pucker, but great as a refreshment. Rich in complex B vitamins, iron and has natural soothing properties.

CANA- SUGAR CANE

The sweetest of all things on God's green earth. Always squeezed on the spot for best flavor.

ABACATE - AVOCADO

Thick and creamy, avocado milk shake; has the largest number of nutrients and vitamins. Great for breakfast.

CAJÚ- CASHEW

Sweet and refreshing with a very distinguished taste and smell. Rich in vitamin A, C and complex B.

ACEROLA

The king of vitamin C (each has more Vim. C than 40 lemons), acerola juice is refreshing and slightly citric.

ACAÍ

Blended together with guarana, acai shakes (or very thick smoothies, if you will) should be consumed with a spoon, and optionally a side of granola for sprinkling. Very caloric yet rich in proteins, fiber, Vitamin E, minerals and a natural cholesterol controller.

o try any of these fruits, you can either go straight to the source and visit the produce market, open
very weekday from 8am to 4pm at Feira de São Joaquim, or you can visit any of the juice bars sprin-
led throughout the city (most popular ones are Sucos 24hr and Fabrica de Sucos, in Barra).

COCO - COCONUT WATER

he best
hing when
ou are de-
ydrating
nder the
un. Drink 2
o cure your
angover.
Rich in min-
rals, potassium, and sodium.

FRUTA DO CONDE

Ugly on
the outside
(looks like
a grenade),
sweet on
the inside.
Talk about
philosophi-
cal dualities! Vitamin C and
complex B.

CARAMBOLA

Star shaped
football with a
juicy and citro-
ny zing. Great
as fruit or in
juice form.

GUARANÁ

Sold normally
n refreshment
orm (refres-
co), guarana
ould be con-
sidered a dis-
ant cousin of
he root beer,
but, just like every juice in Brazil, a lot sweeter. A stimulant
and digestion facilitator. And
dig this: clinically proven to en-
hance sexual performance.

JABUTI-
CABA

A distant
cousin of the
grape, yet
sweeter and
thicker. Great
in fruit form,
specially

when frozen. Bite, spit the seed
and skin out. Rich in complex B
vitamins.

MATE

Slightly caffeined herb used to
make iced tea with a deep and
rich flavor.

PITANGA

Healthy
fruit with
citrony yet
milky taste.
Rich in cal-
cium, iron
and phos-
phorus. A natural stimulant and
anti-diarrhea.

CAJA

A creamy
sweet cousin
of the mango,
not by blood but
by virtue.

CACAO (COCOA FRUIT)

The cocoa
fruit has the
cocoa beans
in the middle,
used to make
chocolate.
The shell is
a fruit, very
sweet and creamy, great in juice
form.

GIFT IDEAS

When window shopping, you will notice things like "4X" preceding the price. This means that the actual price is 4 times the number following it. This is because most stores will lay-away, even cheap stuff like shoes or books.

YOURSELF

Brazilian instruments

Great decoration pieces. Found at: Pelourinho

Brazilian Music CDs

Djavan CD, great for love making. Tom Jobim for after sex music.
Shopping da Barra

Video Hobby Mega Store
Av. Euclides da Cunha 22, Graça

Shoes & Clothes

Brazil is a big player on the international shoe market, due to cheap labor and leather. You can find Italian-design men's shoes for less than US$40, and women's shoes at even cheaper prices.
Vero
Rua Alm. Marques Leao, Barra
Shopping Iguatemi
Large variety of shops and brands

Pestle and mortar

For giving a caipirinha party after you get back from your trip. Found at: Malls

Leather products

Found at: Mercado Modelo

FAMILY

Coffee-table books of Brazil, Salvador etc.

Video Hobby Mega Store
Av. Euclides da Cunha 22, Graça

A jar of doce de leite.

Kids will love it.

Found at: Supermarket

Peppers

Jar of Brazilian peppers, (for display only, never to be used). Found at: Pelourinho

Woven-straw slippers.

Very zen. Found at: Feira Hippie

Brazilian tribal masks

Great decoration piece.
Doidao Bahia
Alameda do Sol in Praia do Forte or
Rua Ana Neri 42 - Centro, Cachoeira

GUY FRIENDS

Brazilian soccer team shirt.

Found at: Pelourinho

Cachaca

Take as many bottles and hope that customs don't confiscate them. Found at supermarkets

Bahian cigars

Bahian cigars are winning acceptance in the international market, due to it's selection of leaves and superior manufacturing quality. Look for Suerdik and Quiteria.
Corona Tabacco
AeroClube Shopping Mall
Airport
Shopping da Barra Mall

LADY-FRIENDS

Jewelry

Lauritano Jewels
Rua das Laranjeiras 52, Pelourinho

Hand-Bags

Shopping da Barra
Mostly fashion brands
Vero
Rua Alm. Marques Leao, Barra

Handcrafted jewelry

Mercado Modelo

Pelourinho

Leather Jewelry box

Mercado Modelo

What's the

Poor people in rich areas

They come to nicer neighborhoods to beg from the rich (which makes sense), but donation is not recommended unless they have a condition. Many of the beggars in working conditions choose to beg. Don't give them anything, as this doesn't help anybody.

Flanelinhas

These are shines that watch your car for a few R$. Each owns a block, and is responsible for whatever happens to your car. Since that is where they will permanently work for a few years, should something go missing, you can find them the next day, and open a can of whoop-ass.

Street vendors everywhere

Selling mostly stuff made in China, street vendors account for about 1/3 of Brazil's work force. This type of business is illegal but frequently overlooked, as most escape the regulating police.

Beach vendors

Just like the street vendors, the beach vendors tend to offer more practical stuff like snacks, ice cream, beer or sunglasses. Forget the hammock guy.

Dog TV

These are rotisserie chicken ovens, often referred to as television for dogs. For around R$8 you can get a chicken cut up for you to take home.

Reckless driving

Since most Brazilians bought their license, or forgot most of the rules and regulations, everyone drives like its Super Nintendo. Interestingly, every year there is one traffic law which is fashionable to follow. This year it is not to stop at pedestrian crossing stripes. All the other rules are ignored.

Blowing stoplights at night:

For safety reasons, most people slow down at red lights, check for traffic, then speed up again, as stopping at a red light in the dark can be dangerous, due to car robbing.

DEAL WITH...

LACK OF TRIBES

Where are the punks? The Nerds? The Hippies? The heroin addicts? The grungy? Salvador doesn't have any visible amount of any of the above. It is mostly preppies, jiu-jitsu fighters (pit bulls), artsy-fartsy (neo-hippies) and normal people. You can find all those other tribes in São Paulo.

EXCESSIVE WAITERS

Given that the minimum wage is R$200 (US$70), most businesses can afford to hire a large staff to improve service. Unfortunately, most of this staff is undertrained, which in effects lowers the quality of service.

HOT WOMEN BY THE SIDE OF THE ROAD?

The tall, hot prostitutes are state-of-the-art transvestites or transsexuals. Don't fall in love.

YOUNG PEOPLE HANGING OUT IN GAS STATIONS

Gas stations became a gathering place for different groups to hang around, blast music and sip beer, probably because they are one of the few convenient stores at open at night.

WHAT'S THE DEAL WITH CONSUMING BEER ANYWHERE?

I know, isn't it great?

THE LACK OF BMWS AND LUXURY CARS?

Brazilians get a 100% tariff on imported cars, so a BMW325e goes for about US$60K. And given that most rich Brazilians don't want to make themselves a visible target for car-jackers, most members of the upper class prefer to drive regular cars.

EUROPEANS RUNNING MOST OF THE TOURISM ESTABLISHMENTS?

Most came here. fell in love and wanted to stay. After finding a niche in the tourism sector (there are still plenty available), they started their thing, and most have succeeded.

If you are interested in moving to Brazil or acquiring real-estate before the market awakens, or to inquire about getting Brazilian residency, contact Doug Simon, a specialist in this area:

Douglas Simon
dsimonbr@yahoo.com or visit bahia-property.com

OVER-PACKED EVENTS?

If you don't like people intruding into your personal space, you should avoid Salvador altogether. All you need is a little music and a beer vendor to turn any event into a major feast.

If it's free, half the city will be there. If someone famous is performing, the entire city. Be ready for moving through the crowd like food through intestines.

BAHIA AT A GLANCE

CHAPADA DIAMANTINA

- *Lençóis* 👍👍👍 ECO TOUR
- *Igatu*
- *Mucugé*

- *Praia do Forte*
  👍👍👍 BEACH AND ECO TOUR

SALVADOR
  👍👍👍👍 BEACH AND ECO TOU
- *Morro de São Paulo*
  👍👍👍 BEACH AND PARTY
- *Itacaré*
  👍👍👍 BEACH

There are two ways to extend your vacation in Brazil: one way is to visit the various tourist spots in the state of Bahia; the other is to take a plane or bus to other popular touristic destinations. If you intend on coming back on future trips to different parts of Brazil, we highly recommend you to stay in Bahia. It offers a little of everything Brazil is known to offer: parties (Porto Seguro), beaches (Itacare, Caravelas), wilderness (Chapada Diamantina) and colonial history (Ilheus). Given Bahia is the size of France, some of these spots can take up to 12 hours to get to, whether by bus or car. All these destinations have proper tourism infrastructure (safety, english spoken, various styles of lodging, tour guides etc.)

- *Porto Seguro* 👍👍👍👍👍 PAR
- *Arraial D'Ajuda* 👍👍👍👍 P
- *Trancoso* 👍👍👍 BEACH

- *Caravelas* 👍👍👍 BEACH AND SCUBA

ATLANTIC OCEA

BRAZIL AT A GLANCE

If you plan on visiting other parts of Brazil, your first stop should be Rio de Janeiro, the marvelous city. If you do, be sure to get a copy of Rio For Partiers (www.rioforpartiers.com). A very popular option is to rent a car and drive north from Salvador, stopping at the various state capitals (Recife&Olinda, Maceio, Natal & Joao Pessoa) and fishermen villages in between. Fernado de Noronha has some of the most beautiful beaches in the world, as well as an incredibly well kept sea life, ideal for divers. Porto Seguro is among the best party towns in the southern hemisphere. Another option during the summer is to hop over to Floranopolis, then to Garopaba and its neighboring towns. This is surfer&babes paradise. If you want to see jungle, people have been having fuller experiences in Bonito and in the Pantanal than the Amazon. You get closer to the animals, you see more and you have more activities to partake.

Fortaleza 🌶🌶🌶 Beach & Party

Manaus 🌶🌶🌶🌶 Amazon Ecotourism

Beach & scuba heaven 🌶🌶🌶🌶 Fernando de Noronha

Dunes Ecotourism 🌶🌶🌶 João Pessoa

Recife 🌶🌶🌶🌶 Culture & Beach

Salvador 🌶🌶🌶🌶🌶 Culture & Party

Porto Seguro 🌶🌶🌶🌶🌶 Party Town

Brasilia 🌶🌶 Architecture

Bonito 🌶🌶🌶🌶 Ecotourism

Ouro Preto 🌶🌶🌶🌶 Culture & Party

Rio de Janeiro 🌶🌶🌶🌶🌶

São Paulo 🌶🌶 Business & Party

Foz do Iguacu 🌶🌶🌶 Waterfalls

Florianopolis 🌶🌶🌶🌶🌶 Beach & Party Town

Porto Alegre 🌶🌶 Party Town

TRAVEL LOG

DATE	DAYTIME ACTIVITY	LUNCH/DINNER	NIGHTTIME ACTIVITY

People I`ve Met Contact List

Date/Place	Name	Email	Notes/Photo#

STREET PRICE GUIDE

All prices in Brazilian Reals $

STREET FOOD ESTIMATOR

Beer 1.50 to 2.50

Acaraje 1 to 3

Hot dog 1 to 3.50

Cheeseburger 1.50 to 3

Juice 1.20 to 3

Water bottle (1/2 liter) 1

Soft drink 1 to 2

Food by the pound 1.30 to 2.40 per 100 grams

Ice cream 1 to 6

Popsicle 0.50 to 1.90

Salgadinho (snack) 1 to 2.50

Straight Coffee 0.50 to 1

Chocolate bar 0.70 to 1.50

Salted Peanut cone 0.50 to 1

Caipirinha 3 to 6

Crab 2 to 4

SERVICES

Chair at the beach 1.50 to 3

Umbrella 2 to 3

Bike rental 4 to 15 per hour

Bike rental 20 to 50 per day

Artistic cover for live music bars 3 to 15

Beach massage 40 1/2 hour

Internet access 4 to 10 per hour

Prostitute 3 to 300 (really!)

TAXI FARE ESTIMATOR

As a rule, estimate $1 per minute of taxi ride without traffic, 0.80 per minute with heavy traffic. Add 20% for night time rides (after 9pm) or Sundays:

From Pelourinho to:

Barra - 12

Rio Vermelho - 15

Aeroclube - 27

Casquinha - 40

Boca Do Rio - 30

Itapuã - 40

Aeroporto - 45

Ribeira - 15

From Barra to:

Rio Vermelho - 9

Aeroclube - 20

Casquinha - 30

Boca Do Rio - 24

Itapuã - 35

Aeroporto - 40

Ribeira - 20

From Rio Vermelho to:

Aeroclube - 15

Casquinha - 25

Boca Do Rio - 19

Itapuã - 30

Aeroporto - 35

Ribeira - 24

If you get rates double the above -mentioned prices, or it seems extremely unfair, step out the taxi, call the nearest cop and tell him "o taximetro esta desregulado", meaning the meter has been tampered with. Write down their licence plate and send it to me. cris@salvadorforpartiers.com

STREET VENDORS ESTIMATOR

Fake sunglasses 5 to 15

Fake cap 10 to 20

Fake Brazilian soccer team shirt 20 to 40

Fake music CD 5 to 10

Fake software CD 10 to 15

Fake movie 10 to 15

Beach canga 8 to 20

Postcard 0.50 to 3

PRICES ESTIMATOR

Bus from Salvador to: Porto Seguro = $90, Praia do Forte =$12, Chapada Diamantina=$80 or Itacare=$50

Flight to: Rio=$500, Fortaleza= $300, Brasilia= $200 or Recife = $160 each way

One night hardcore clubbing (10 drinks) = $90

One very nice dinner (contemporary cuisine, drinks and dessert)= R$60pp